Sudo Mastery

2nd Edition

Michael W Lucas

Tilted Windmill Press

Sudo Mastery, 2nd Edition
Copyright 2019 by Michael W Lucas (https://mwl.io).

All rights reserved.

Author: Michael W Lucas
Copyediting: Amanda Robinson
Cover art: Eddie Sharam, "A Mascot in Need," after John Phillip's "A Friend in Need," 1857.

ISBN (paperback): 978-1-64235-030-2
ISBN (hardcover): 978-1-64235-031-9

All rights reserved. No part of this work may be reproduced or transmitted in any form or by any means, electronic or mechanical, including but not limited to photocopying, recording, engraving on the surface of Io, or by any information storage or retrieval system, without the prior written permission of the copyright holder and the publisher. For information on book distribution, translations, or other rights, please contact Tilted Windmill Press (accounts@tiltedwindmillpress.com).

The information in this book is provided on an "As Is" basis, without warranty. While every precaution has been taken in the preparation of this work, neither the author nor Tilted Windmill Press shall have any liability to any person or entity with respect to any loss or damage caused or alleged to be caused directly or indirectly by the information contained in it.

Tilted Windmill Press
https://www.tiltedwindmillpress.com

Sudo Mastery
2nd Edition

Michael W Lucas

More Tech Books from Michael W Lucas

Absolute BSD
Absolute OpenBSD (1st and 2nd edition)
Cisco Routers for the Desperate (1st and 2nd edition)
PGP and GPG
Absolute FreeBSD (2nd and 3rd edition)
Network Flow Analysis

the IT Mastery Series

SSH Mastery (1st and 2nd edition)
DNSSEC Mastery
Sudo Mastery
FreeBSD Mastery: Storage Essentials
Networking for Systems Administrators
Tarsnap Mastery
FreeBSD Mastery: ZFS
FreeBSD Mastery: Specialty Filesystems
FreeBSD Mastery: Advanced ZFS
PAM Mastery
Relayd and Httpd Mastery
Ed Mastery
FreeBSD Mastery: Jails

Novels (as Michael Warren Lucas)

Immortal Clay
Kipuka Blues
Butterfly Stomp Waltz
Terrapin Sky Tango
Hydrogen Sleets
git commit murder

Brief Contents

Acknowledgements 15

Chapter 0: Introduction 17

Chapter 1: Sudo Essentials 33

Chapter 2: Managing Sudoers 43

Chapter 3: Lists and Aliases 53

Chapter 4: Options and Defaults 75

Chapter 5: Shell Escapes, Editing, and Policies 83

Chapter 7: Configuring Sudo 93

Chapter 8: Environments 99

Chapter 9: Intrusion Detection 121

Chapter 10: Policy Distribution 133

Chapter 11: Security Policies in LDAP 147

Chapter 12: Logging, Mail, and Debugging 167

Chapter 13: Authentication 185

Afterword 203

Sponsors 205

Patronizers 207

Complete Contents

Acknowledgements 15

Chapter 0: Introduction 17
    What Is Sudo? 20
    What's Wrong with Sudo? 21
    What Does Sudo Protect You From? 23
    Sudo Terms and Support 23
    Prerequisites 24
    Who Should Read This Book? 25
    Learning Sudo 27
    Avoiding Sudo 28
        What Groups Am I In? 29
        Programs versus Groups 29
    Eliminating Root 29
    Book Overview 31

Chapter 1: Sudo Essentials 33
    sudo 101 33
        Sudo Features 34
        Running Commands as Another User 35
        Running Commands as Another Group 36
        Changing Usernames but Keeping Your Groups 37
        Viewing Your Sudo Privileges 37
    Reading Sudoers 37
        Multiple Entries 39
        Permitting Commands as Other Users 40
    Special Characters 41
    Reading the Policy 42

Chapter 2: Managing Sudoers 43
    Creating Sudoers 44
    Visudo Editors 45
    Testing and Verifying Sudoers 47
        User Access Testing 47
        Testing for Automation and Distribution 48
    Including Files in Sudoers 50
        Including Individual Files 50

    Including Directories 51
Chapter 3: Lists and Aliases 53
    Wildcards 53
        Matching Individual Numbers and Characters 54
        Matching Directories...55
        Matching Everything...55
        Wildcard Dangers 56
        Blocking Everything 57
    Aliases 57
    User Lists and Aliases 59
        Operating System Groups..60
        User ID 60
        Group ID 61
        Netgroup 61
        Non-Unix Group..62
        Non-Unix Group ID 62
        User Aliases 62
    Hosts, Host Lists and Aliases 63
        IP Addresses 63
        Netgroups..64
        Host Aliases 64
    RunAs Lists and Aliases 65
        RunAs Lists...65
        RunAs Aliases...66
    Command Lists and Aliases 66
        Command Aliases..67
        Command Tags 67
    Excess Rules 68
        The Command Alias "ALL" Is Dangerous............................68
        Allowing All Legitimate Commands....................................69
    Negation in Lists...71
    Aliases in sudo(8)..73

Chapter 4: Options and Defaults...75
    Defaults...75
    Option Types 76
        Boolean Options 76

- Integer Options 77
  - Integers Usable in a Boolean Context 77
  - String Options 78
- Setting Options for Specific Contexts 78
  - Per-User Defaults 78
  - Per-Host Defaults..79
  - Per-Command Defaults 80
- Per RunAs Defaults 81
- Conflicting Defaults...81
- Options and Lists 82

Chapter 5: Shell Escapes, Editing, and Policies 83
- Forbidding Commands from Executing Commands 84
- Editing Files 87
  - Configuring Sudoedit 88
  - Using Sudoedit 88
  - Symlinks and Directory Ownership................................88
- Policies and Commands..89

Chapter 7: Configuring Sudo 93
- Sudo's Default Configuration 93
- sudo.conf 94
- Sudo Core Dumps..96
- Plugins 96
  - Plugin Path...97
  - Installing Plugins 97
- Configuring the Sudoers Policy 98

Chapter 8: Environments 99
- Sudo-Specific Environment Variables.................................99
- Dangerous Environment Variables 100
- Execution Environment 101
- Environment Variable Filtering..102
  - Preserving Environment Variables 102
  - Sanitizing Environment Variables 103
  - Sudo's Standard Shell Environment..............................104
  - Keep Nothing 104
  - Setting the Environment for One Rule 105
- Retaining the User Environment 105

    Discarding Environment Variables 106
    Environment Option Priority 106
  Allowing User Overrides...107
  Target User Environment..108
  Environment Customization 110
    Adding Environment Variables..110
    Managing PATH 111
    Managing HOME 112
    Managing Pagers 112
  Running Shells with Sudo 113
  Terminals and Graphic Interfaces...115
    No Terminal...115
    Requiring a Terminal 116
    Backgrounding Commands 117
  Timeouts...117
    Timeouts as Soft Policy Enforcement 118
    User Timeouts 119

Chapter 9: Intrusion Detection...121
  Digest Algorithm..122
  Generating Digests...122
  Digests in Sudoers..123
  Multiple Operating Systems 124
  Automating Checksum-Aware Sudoers..124
    Creating Command Aliases with Checksums 125
    Creating a Master Alias...128
    Custom Aliases..130
    Putting It All Together 131

Chapter 10: Policy Distribution..133
  Global Policy Hints..133
  Hostnames and Sudoers...136
    DNS and Sudoers..136
    IP Addresses 138
  One Network, One Sudoers...139
  Transforming and Filtering Sudoers..140
    A Sample Policy 140
    cvtsudoers Output Format..142

  Filtering by Host, User, or Group 142
  Expanding Aliases..144
  The cvtsudoers Config File 145

Chapter 11: Security Policies in LDAP 147
 Prerequisites..148
 The Sudo Schema..150
  Adding Sudo to Traditional OpenLDAP 150
  OpenLDAP with Online Configuration 150
  Adding Sudo to Active Directory 151
 The Policy Container 151
 LDAP Sudo Policies versus Sudoers 151
 Transforming Sudoers to LDIF 153
  Sudo Rules in LDIF...155
 Sudo Rules and Roles...156
  sudoUser 157
  sudoHost 157
  sudoCommand..158
  sudoOption..158
  sudoRunAsUser 159
  sudoRunAsGroup 159
  sudoOrder..159
 Activating LDAP in sudo(8) 160
  Finding the LDAP Policy 160
  Tell sudo To Use LDAP 162
 Disabling Sudoers 162
 Migrations and Learning SudoRoles 163
 LDAP Caching...164

Chapter 12: Logging, Mail, and Debugging..................................167
 Syslog 167
  Customizing Sudo Syslog...168
  Syslog Security...169
 Email 170
  Sending Mail..170
  Setting Email Conditions...171
  Mail Tags 171
  Debugging Sudo and Sudoers 172

    Subsystems and Levels 172
    Configuring Debug Logging 173
    Debug Usefulness..174
  Complete Session Logging..174
    I/O Log Directory 175
    Enabling I/O Logging..176
    Listing I/O Logs 177
    Viewing Individual Sessions...178
    Altering Playback...179
    Real Time Logging...180
    Searching I/O Logs 180
    I/O Log Rotation..183

Chapter 13: Authentication..185
  Password Management and Failure 185
    Password Attempts and Timeouts 185
  Alternate Passwords..186
    Failure Responses..187
  Customizing the Password Prompt 188
    Custom Prompts via Policy 188
    User Prompt Customization..189
  Effective and Expiration Dates..190
  Selectively Disabling Authentication..191
  Authentication Caching and Timeouts..193
    Configuring Timeouts..193
    Erasing Timeouts 194
    Multi-Session Authentication 194
    Authentication, Updates, and Queries.......................................195
  Lecturing Users 196
  PAM and Sudo...197
    Prerequisites 198
    Configuring PAM 199
    authorized_keys Location..201

Afterword 203

Sponsors..205

Patronizers..207

"The first edition isn't pining, it's passed on! The edition is no more! It has ceased usefulness! It's gone to meet the recycler! It's remaindered! Bereft of readers, it rests in peace! THIS… is an ex-book!"

Acknowledgements

There are many reasons to do a second edition of *Sudo Mastery*: the replacement of sudo2ldif with cvtsudoers, new options, changes in the technology environment, and my own deeper understanding of sudo. Honesty compels me to confess that sudo's addition of Monty Python insults, giving me an opportunity to start each chapter with a mangled Python quote, probably weighed more heavily in this decision than it should have. The person who helped me come up with the quotes, there are some who call him… Tim.

Before publication, this book was reviewed for technical accuracy by Ron Collinson, Trix Farrar, Thomas Harrison, Dwayne Hart, Ed Neville, Daniele Palumbo, Carsten Strotmann, and Grant Taylor. While I appreciate my technical reviewers, all errors in this book are mine. Reviewers who want blame for errors should go make their own.

Thanks also to Todd Miller, who has the Sisyphean task of maintaining sudo across dozens of platforms.

XKCD fans should note that the author does not particularly enjoy sandwiches. Miod Vallat, currently comfortably ensconced in France, would really like a sandwich with nice fresh bread, really good mustard, and low-carb ground glass and rusty nails. It's unlikely that I'll get to France any time this decade, so if you could help him out I'd appreciate it.

I apologize for the fault in the book design. Those responsible have been sacked. The chapters have been numbered in an entirely different style at great expense and at the last minute.

For Liz.

"He's not root, he's a very naughty boy."

Chapter 0: Introduction

Resolved: controlling a user's access to a computer's privileged programs and files is a right pain. The few systems that could more or less cope with mapping real-world privileges onto digital schemes didn't survive. The best access control systems in popular operating systems merely inflict less torment than the others.

The most widespread operating system these days is Unix, which controls programs and file access through users and groups. Each individual user has a unique username, and usernames are arranged into uniquely named groups. Specific users and groups get permission to access specific files and programs. This scheme was developed decades ago, when a large university might have a couple of UNIX servers. Hundreds of users logged onto each server for mail, Usenet, and other computation-heavy applications. Students went in one group, grad students in another, then professors, staff, and so on. Individual classes and departments might have their own groups.

Among all those accounts, `root` is special. The `root` account has ultimate control of the system. To protect the host, Unix restricts some programs so that only `root` can run them. Only `root` can reconfigure the network, mount filesystems, and restart programs that attach to privileged network ports. Only `root` can add new users. This made sense when a whole university campus might have only one or two computers—reconfiguring the network or adding storage is a serious task in that environment. Management of multimillion-dollar systems that thousands of people rely on should remain in trusted, skilled hands.

Today, instead of a single UNIX™ we have untold Unixes, several BSDs, innumerable Linuxes, and similar-but-not-quite-Unixy variants. For ease of reference I'll call the whole family "Unix," even though that's not strictly accurate. Anyone reading this introduction probably has a few Unixes in their home and one on their belt. Teams of people might share sysadmin tasks, or one person might completely control each system, or anything in between. Our security requirements are completely different from twentieth-century universities.

Large organizations with many servers often divide sysadmin responsibilities between skilled individuals. One person might be responsible for the care and feeding of the operating system, while a second person handles the server's primary application. The server supports the application, and the application is the reason the server exists. Both people must perform tasks that require root-level privileges.

The problem is, **root** access is all-or-nothing. Unix doesn't differentiate between "access to change the kernel" and "access to install and upgrade applications in */opt*." An application administrator with **root** access can change the kernel and adjust filesystems.

Many small teams rely on gentleman's agreements to only touch the parts of the system each person is responsible for. Such agreements decay exponentially with the number of people involved. Two people can just about keep things straight. Once you have a sysadmin team and a DBA team, such agreements start off with finger-pointing and devolve into bloodbaths. Sometimes the resulting debacles are not the fault of anyone in the organization; I've seen more than one disaster trace back to a vendor-provided script that committed unspeakable acts upon a helpless server.

Organizations need finer-grained access control than **root** provides.

The all-or-nothing model breaks down even more when everyone has a Unix system. Setting aside the innumerable phones and tablets specifically engineered for user-friendliness, many of us run Unix on a desktop or laptop. Every time you access a USB drive or use a coffee shop wireless network, something on the system needs root-level privileges. Becoming root isn't terribly onerous on your own system—log in as yourself, use su(1) to switch users, enter the root password, run your privileged commands, and exit the root account. Performing this ritual every time you put in a USB drive, bounce the network, restart or reconfigure software, or install new packages gets annoying. Add-on tools like automounters and network managers help, but configuring them requires—wait for it—**root** privileges.

The computer industry is full of really smart people who have expanded the classic Unix access control model. One method is through *setuid* and *setgid* programs. While programs normally work with the privileges of the user who runs them, setuid and setgid set their effective user and group ID to some other user. Many setuid programs run as **root**. Changing your password requires editing secure files in /etc, so passwd(1) is setuid root. Intruders really like setuid and setgid programs, and gleefully exploit any flaws in them to achieve illicit **root** access. Most programmers don't have the level of skill needed to truly lock down setuid and setgid programs, and on some platforms such security is nearly impossible. Additionally, most operating systems don't let you make shell scripts setuid.

We also have several varieties of *access control list* (ACL) that more broadly expand the user-group-others ownership model. ACLs allow you to set highly customized file and command ownership. "This person owns the file, but these people and these groups—except for these folks, unless they're specifically given permission earlier—can modify it, and these other people and groups—with their own exclusions—can execute it, while read access is restricted to these people and groups…" And of course, all these different ACL implementations are ever so slightly incompatible. NFSv4 ACLs were designed to be interoperable with Microsoft's NTFS ACLs. The specification is over 107,000 words long—and they still didn't manage complete compatibility. At this point the sysadmin starts contemplating a career cleaning up real sewage instead of the metaphorical kind. Very few people can implement ACLs on a single platform, and deep expertise in one ACL system isn't completely applicable to other platforms. ACLs have a place in systems administration, and they're invaluable if you really *need* them. But most of us try really, really hard not to need them.

Sadly, access control lists are about as good as it gets.

That's why the world has settled on sudo.

What Is Sudo?

Sudo is a program that allows conditional escalation of user privilege. The system owner creates a list of commands that each user can run. When the user wants to run a command that requires root, he asks sudo(8) to run the command for him. Sudo consults its permissions list. If the list grants the user permission to run that command, sudo runs the command as **root**. If the user does not have permission to run the command, sudo informs him. Running sudo does not require the root password, but rather the user's own authentication credentials. (SUSE Linux uses a special configuration to require the root password for sudo, but they're the exception.)

Sudo lets the sysadmin delegate root privileges to specific people for very specific tasks. She can tell sudo to require authentication for some users or commands and not for others, or only on certain machines, all with one configuration file.

Many enterprise software suites, like PostgreSQL, require running commands under a specific dedicated account. Users must switch to this account before managing certain core functions. You can configure sudo to permit users access to this account, or to only permit them to run certain specific commands as this user. Maybe your junior DBA needs access to dump the database, while the lead DBA needs a full-on shell prompt as the database account. Sudo lets you do that.

Finally, sudo logs everything everybody asks it to do. It can even record the contents of individual sudo sessions, showing you exactly who broke what.

What's Wrong with Sudo?

If sudo is so great, why doesn't everybody use it?

Sudo adds another layer of system administration. That layer demands time, energy, and attention. It requires learning yet another danged program when you already have too much to do. If you're responsible for running an organization with several groups of administrators, investing in learning and deploying sudo will dramatically reduce your workload and inter-group problems.

Some commercial Unixes don't include sudo because they use their own proprietary privilege management system. OpenSolaris-based systems have pfexec(1) and role-based access control (RBAC), which is both superior to sudo and more complicated. HP/UX had pbrun(1). Many others were sold to the unwitting as "improvements over sudo" and are probably still in use all around the world. If you were a commercial Unix software vendor who seriously invested in developing an

ACL-based privilege management system, would you support using a simpler, easier tool? I would, but that's yet another reason why I'm not a commercial Unix vendor.

You'll also see simpler privilege escalation tools such as OpenBSD's doas(1). If those tools meet your needs, use them. If your organization demands features such as LDAP integration or using the single master configuration, though, you'll need to implement sudo.

Many Unixes include sudo in their base system. Some, such as Ubuntu and macOS, completely disable the root account and permit privileged access via sudo. This is a lurch in the right direction, but most people who have sudo use it incorrectly.

What's the wrong way to use sudo? Sudo is not merely a replacement for su(1). Sudo is not a way to avoid requiring authentication for privileged access. Sudo is not a tool to force someone to make you a sandwich, despite the famous XKCD comic. A proper sudo setup simplifies system management. An improper sudo setup makes it faster and easier for intruders to corrupt or destroy your system, or too easy for you to accidentally wipe your laptop.

"Proper use of sudo" doesn't mean complicated or extensive policies. I've seen system administrators spend hours writing intricate sudo policies, only to watch users waltz right past their restrictions—often without realizing that the restrictions were in place. Sudo has limits and edges. Once you understand those limits, you can make realistic decisions about how and where your organization deploys sudo.

The sudo problem I see most often has nothing to do with the software. A proper sudo deployment in a complicated organization requires the various sysadmin teams to agree who is responsible for what. Sudo enforces job duties and responsibilities in a configuration file. The configuration file is flexible, but people cannot exceed the permissions specified therein.

What are the boundaries of your responsibilities? What permissions do you truly need to perform your assigned work, and which tasks should someone else do? Being forced to sit down and discuss these matters temporarily increases the bickering within an organization. Once the arguments settle, however, conflicts decrease. Everybody knows that the database team can't format filesystems, the web team can't restart the database, and every privileged keystroke is logged. The audit trail improves system stability and makes everyone's lives easier.

When people know that they can and will be held responsible for breaking things, they stop breaking things so often. Weird.

What Does Sudo Protect You From?

Sudo protects the system from harm by intruders or sysadmins, and it protects sysadmins from many management problems.

Giving a user access to a limited set of privileged commands limits the damage the user can inflict on the system. The user who can only manage web servers cannot mangle disk partitions. If an intruder compromises that user's account, that intruder will be slowed or even contained.

Similarly, lack of access protects the sysadmin when something fails. Even without sudo logs, a user with limited access can say "I didn't fry the database partition, I don't have that access." Accountability works both ways. Use it to your advantage.

Sudo Terms and Support

Sudo is freely available open source software. You are welcome to download it from https://sudo.ws and use it throughout your organization at no charge. The BSD-style license has only two terms: don't use sudo's name to promote yourself, and don't sue us if it breaks. You can use sudo as the basis of your own products, resell it, or incorporate it into software you then redistribute or sell. You can even deploy it throughout your multibillion-dollar firm at no charge.

What you don't get is sophisticated support.

Sudo is not released by a commercial company. It's developed and supported by the users who need it, coordinated for many years now by Todd Miller. You can contribute to sudo by submitting patches and bug reports. Third parties will support your sudo install or even write custom code for you. But there's nobody to yell at if your sudo install doesn't work the way you expect. There is no toll-free number answered by a flunky with a dubious grasp of your language being paid minimum wage to exchange your abuse and invective for meaningless platitudes.

Having said that, the folks on the sudo mailing list and many operating-system-specific forums and mailing lists are both helpful and interested in real problem reports. They respond well to requests and poorly to demands. If you want to demand help—if you want to scream and rant and rave and turn blue until your problem goes away—any number of companies and consultants will sell you that.

The software is free. Sudo's official support is a gift that evaporates the second you stop treating it like one.

Prerequisites

This book assumes you're running sudo on a Unix operating system. Sudo is available for BSD, macOS, Linux, OpenSolaris derivatives, and every existing commercial Unix. It also runs on Minix. I tested my examples on FreeBSD 12, Centos 7, and Debian 9.9, and I'll mention other Unixes in passing.

Check the version of sudo on your host by running `sudo -V`. While this book's reference implementation is sudo 1.8.27 and creeping towards 1.8.28, you should always run the latest version of sudo. A surprising number of operating system packagers include wildly obsolete sudo versions, which might include security flaws. As I write this FreeBSD ships with sudo 1.8.27, CentOS with 1.8.23, and Debian with 1.8.19. Operating system packagers who ship obsolete software declare that they backport all critical security fixes to their packages, but you're better off installing the latest. Get the latest releases, both in source form and precompiled for a variety of Unixes, at https://sudo.ws.

This book uses pure sudo, with mostly default compiler options. (I had to add LDAP support to document LDAP, for example.) Some operating system packagers change sudo's defaults to fit more closely with their vision, and update those changes far more frequently than I release new editions of this book. Watch out for places where your packager varied from the standard.

The sudo documentation and this book both assume that your operating system conforms fairly closely to tradition. My examples show commands in standard directories such as `/bin`, `/usr/bin`, `/sbin`, and so on. If your Unix uses its own directory layout, adjust the examples to match.

Who Should Read This Book?

Everyone who works on a Unix system should understand sudo.

Sysadmins responsible for other users need to assign those users exactly the privileges needed to do their jobs, no more and no less. Correct sudo configuration frees up your time and protects the system from well-intentioned disasters.

Application administrators, you just want to do your job. This means you need access to perform privileged tasks. Working via sudo means slightly changing your processes—not in any major way, but you can go completely bonkers trying to figure out why `sudo cd` doesn't work until you understand what's happening. An understanding of sudo lets you draft the sudo rules you need and provide them to your sysadmin. Even if she disagrees, negotiating in sudo policy language means that everyone understands exactly what you're requesting. You can have specific discussions about who is responsible for what. No worthwhile sysadmin will tell you that you don't need access to manage your application—she certainly doesn't want the job![1] The only question is, how can that access be best accomplished?

If a disagreement between teams is broad enough, this is where you invoke management to make a very specific decision and set clear lines of authority and responsibility. In some organizations, getting that manager to take that step is a miracle—but a mandate to implement sudo lets you corner him. And if you have a cranky sysadmin who claims that granting you necessary access without giving you root is impossible, this book will let you categorically refute that. Resolving either of these cases is, admittedly, its own vindictive pleasure.

Why would people who maintain only their personal systems care about sudo? Even on a laptop, some commands merit more thought and consideration than others. It's sensible to trivially reconfigure a laptop's network, tweak removable media, or kill that processor-hogging browser. My fingers configure networks so frequently that they can perform the whole task without disturbing my brain. Tasks you perform less often, such as installing software or formatting disks, merit more focus. It makes sense to configure sudo to transparently allow access to a few basic commands such as ifconfig(8) and mount(8), but to require authentication before using newfs(8) or upgrading.

---

[1] Seasoned sysadmins and experienced application administrators share the exact same goal: to speak with each other as little as possible.

Or maybe you like reinstalling your laptop. Whatever works for you.

While many important Unix programs require an extensive background to understand, sudo is fairly self-contained. You can master sudo without understanding all the programs that users can access via sudo. Sudo is a system management tool, however. The better you understand Unix, the better you can leverage sudo and the more confidence you'll have in your configuration.

Learning Sudo

The official sudo documentation describes the sudo policy language in Extended Backus-Naur Form (EBNF), a formal grammar for program configuration. I won't take you through formal EBNF-style definitions. Instead, this book demonstrates the most important sudo features through configuration snippets and example policies.

Also note that this book does not cover all possible sudo configurations, nor does it cover every possible sudo feature. I cover what the vast majority of sysadmins need, but if you're running an older operating system, an old version of sudo, or something that isn't quite Unix, you'll need to dive into the documentation to identify sudo's sharp edges. But after reading this book you'll have a solid grounding in sudo techniques and a good idea of exactly what information you're looking for and how to use it.

As you configure sudo, remember that enumerating badness always fails. Unix is full of tools that can be cleverly abused, and the combined intelligence of the world's jerks is greater than yours. Listing abusable and exploitable software is a doomed effort. List what people *can* do, rather than what they cannot. We'll keep returning to this point.

Avoiding Sudo

Unix controls access by users, groups, and others. Many sysadmins have a mysterious blind spot about group permissions, preferring to require root privileges rather than configuring a group. Before running to sudo to solve your access control problems, see if you can resolve them with groups instead. Requiring root privileges to permit access to files or programs is like requiring use of a sledgehammer to hang a picture.

Use group permissions to control access to programs or files that must be accessed by several people, and only those people. Assume several people maintain the files for your web site. Create a group called **www** and assign that group ownership of the web site directory and all the files within it. Here's the site's top-level directory.

```
# ls -la
total 487
drwxrwxr-x  3 root   www            6 May 22 16:40 .
drwxrwxrwt  7 root   wheel          7 May 22 16:44 ..
-rw-rw-r--  1 mike   www       436279 Aug  5  2018 banner.jpg
drwxrwxr-x  2 pete   www           46 May 22 16:42 content
-rw-rw-r--  1 thea   www         1988 May 22 16:41 index.php
-rw-rw-r--  1 thea   www        25854 May  1  2015 logo.jpg
```

The individual files are owned by a single account—**mike**, **thea**, or **pete**. The files are also readable and writable by anyone in the group **www**. Anyone in this group can edit these files and the directory below it.

Perhaps you want to make the directory setgid and ensure that all of your users have a umask of 002, so that newly created files get the same group membership. Or maybe these users shouldn't be creating new files, only editing existing ones. Choose your problems.

Most Unixes offer programs like vigr(8) to create and edit groups, or provide programs to change group memberships purely on the command line. Use whatever tool your Unix recommends.

What Groups Am I In?

Use id(1) to list the groups your account is in.
```
$ id
uid=1000(mike) gid=1000(mike) groups=1000(mike),
24(cdrom),25(floppy),29(audio),30(dip),44(video),
46(plugdev),108(netdev),10001(www)
```

My account is in the groups **mike**, **cdrom**, **floppy**, **audio**, **dip**, **video**, **plugdev**, **netdev**, and **www**. As a member of **www**, I could muck with the files shown above. I could also edit the file *banner.jpg* because I own it.

Programs versus Groups

Group permissions don't solve all access problems for programs. Some programs perform privileged functions, and letting a group run the program won't give the program rights to perform the task. Remember, a program runs with the privileges of the person running the program.

The web server runs on ports 80 and 443. Only **root** can attach to network ports below 1024. If a user runs the web server program without any extra privileges, the program will run as that user account. It won't be able to attach to its network ports. Setting */usr/sbin/httpd* to be owned by the group **www** doesn't give that permission. A user in **www** can't start the server even though they can run the program.

If you want the **www** group to get root privileges specifically for starting, stopping, and managing the web server, you must give the group members root privileges. That's where sudo comes in, letting you assign that group those privileges without allowing them general root access.

Eliminating Root

The goal of this book is to let you replace access to privileged commands via the su(1) command with sudo(8), and the root (or other target user) password with the user's credentials. The root password will become something used only in a disaster, or perhaps when you're at the physical console. The best way to fail in this attempt is to deploy sudo too quickly.

Configuring sudo has its own pitfalls. You'll need to learn how sudo fits into your environment. Nothing beats locking yourself out of your own server for agonized self-recrimination. Don't be too quick to disable root access via su(1), as you can use that access to repair a broken sudo configuration. Yes, sudo has tools to verify that your sudo policy is syntactically correct. A sudo policy that says "nobody can do anything" is syntactically correct, however. Leave your old root access in place until you are utterly confident in either the new sudo arrangements or booting into single-user mode to repair sudo. A virtual machine, chroot, or jail is very useful for destructive learning.

Unixes such as Ubuntu and macOS provide root access with sudo(8) rather than su(1). If you're experimenting with sudo, and sudo is your main method of accessing privileged commands, you're in a risky situation. Before mucking with sudo, give your host a root password. This enables root access with su(1), giving you a path to rescue yourself when you inevitably goof. Test the root password before starting with sudo. Once you're comfortable with sudo, you can choose to disable that root password.

Disabling root password access varies by Unix. On Centos and BSD, users who can use su must be in the **wheel** group. Debian permits anyone who knows the root password to use it; truly disabling su(1) access requires editing */etc/pam.d/su* and enabling one of the commented-out pam_wheel entries.[2]

---

2   You could try keeping the root password a secret, but we all know how well *that* works.

Book Overview

You're just about to finish Chapter 0 right now.

Chapter 1, *Sudo Essentials*, discusses the tools that make up the core of sudo. Sudo is not a single program, but rather a small group of programs.

Chapter 2, *Managing Sudoers*, covers the `sudoers` sudo policy file. You'll learn how to safely edit and test your sudo policy. It won't guarantee that your policy does what you want, but it can verify that your new policy won't break sudo.

Chapter 3, *Lists and Aliases*, demonstrates sudoers syntax designed to simplify your policy.

Chapter 4, *Options and Defaults*, discusses ways to change sudo's behavior.

Chapter 5, *Shell Escapes, Editing, and Policies*, covers some trickier edges of sudo, where users can use standard program features to evade your restrictions unless you take steps to prevent them.

Chapter 7, *Configuring Sudo*, helps you change the way the sudo(8) binary behaves internally, letting you change policy engines or add entirely new features.

Chapter 8, *Environments*, covers how shell environments impact sudo. You can control the environment privileged commands run in, and how much the user can adjust that environment.

Chapter 9, *Intrusion Detection*, discusses how sudo can verify the integrity of binaries before executing them. Sudo can't prevent intrusions, but it can react to them.

Chapter 10, *Policy Distribution*, teaches you how to create a single common policy that you push to all your hosts.

Chapter 11, *Security Policies in LDAP*, shows how to feed your policy to an LDAP server.

Chapter 12, *Logging, Mail, and Debugging*, discusses all three of sudo's logging systems.

Chapter 13, *Authentication*, covers how sudo handles passwords and other authentication data.

But before you jump into the complex stuff, make sure you understand the basics.

"Root? You were lucky to have root! We used to live as operator."

Chapter 1: Sudo Essentials

The most obvious components of the sudo suite are sudo(8) and the *sudoers* policy file. By the time you drag yourself through this book you'll understand the visudo(8) policy-editing command, the cvtsudoers(1) policy-transformation tool, and the sudoreplay(8) log analysis program. Initially, we'll start with the most visible part.

sudo 101

You want to run a privileged command via sudo? Run `sudo` followed by the desired command. Here I want to mount my home directory from the host **bigfileserver**, an operation that normally requires root privileges.

```
$ sudo mount bigfileserver:/home/mike /mnt
We trust you have received the usual lecture from the
local System Administrator. It usually boils down to
these three things:

    #1) Respect the privacy of others.
    #2) Think before you type.
    #3) With great power comes great responsibility.

Password:
```

The first time you run sudo on any host, it prints a message about the importance of not abusing your power and caring for the host. Take this lecture to heart. Privileged commands are privileged because they can reconfigure, deconfigure, damage, demolish, devastate, and destroy operating systems and occasionally the underlying hardware. If you have never received the lecture mentioned any senior sysadmin will oblige, illustrating her tale with several hundred examples.

Sudo then requests a password. It needs your password, not the root password. If you enter your password correctly, and if you have permission to run this command via sudo, you'll get the program's normal output.

```
mount_nfs: bigfileserver: hostname nor servname
    provided, or not known
```

Oh, right. The office sysadmins renamed this fileserver.

The good news is, sudo remembers that you authenticated and will let you run sudo commands in this terminal without further authentication for five minutes. If you want to update this time without running a command, run `sudo -v` to revalidate your session and reset the clock.

You now know as much about sudo as the overwhelming majority of users. Every tip you pick up past this point makes you more of an expert than everyone around you.

Sudo Features

Every operating system packager builds sudo differently. Even minimalist Unixes like FreeBSD turn on PAM and shift everything into `/usr/local` to comply with the operating system standards. Unixes that nail a consistent interface onto everything, like Debian, make more extensive changes. When you work with a new operating system you'll need to check if specific features are enabled. The -V flag tells you the essentials about your sudo. Here I check sudo's features as a regular user.

```
$ sudo -V
Sudo version 1.8.27
Sudoers policy plugin version 1.8.27
Sudoers file grammar version 46
Sudoers I/O plugin version 1.8.27
```

My software is current, as per the sudo home page. But using `-V` as **root** is more interesting.

```
# sudo -V
Sudo version 1.8.27
Configure options: --sysconfdir=/usr/local/etc --with-
ignore-dot --with-tty-tickets --with-env-editor
--with-logincap --with-long-otp-prompt --with-rundir=/
var/run/sudo --with-logfac=authpriv --with-bsm-audit
--enable-nls --disable-noargs-shell --with-pam --pre-
fix=/usr/local --localstatedir=/var --mandir=/usr/local/
man --infodir=/usr/local/share/info/ --build=amd64-port-
bld-freebsd12.0
Sudoers policy plugin version 1.8.27
Sudoers file grammar version 46

Sudoers path: /etc/sudoers
Authentication methods: 'pam'
Syslog facility if syslog is being used for logging:
authpriv
…
```

We see the compile-time flags, as well as the various settings hard-coded into the software (which might well deviate from what sudo ships with, if the OS packager wanted sudo to smell more like the rest of their Unix). If something doesn't work as expected, review this output.

Running Commands as Another User

Maybe you don't want to damage, devastate, or demolish the system. Perhaps you're after a big application server or the database, with a dedicated management user. The application expects to run as that user, and that user's environment is configured to manage the application. Everything from Java Server Pages applications to Ansible uses this configuration. Run a command as that specific user by adding the -u flag. Here I run `psql` as the user **pg**.

sudo -u pg psql

When you authenticate you become the user **pg**, with that user's environment, and run the command. You become that user in all things, including group memberships.

Running Commands as Another Group

Every user has a *primary group*, listed with their account in /etc/passwd. Other groups that the user belongs to, as listed in /etc/group, are considered secondary groups. Some programs only function properly if the user's primary group is its group. Depending on how your operating system handles groups and how the picky command is installed, you might need to change your primary group to use the command. Sudo lets you change your primary group with the -g flag.

$ **sudo -g operator pickycommand**

Sudo lies to the program and tells it that your primary group is **operator**. Your username is unchanged; you run this command as yourself, merely with a different primary group.

Use a group ID number rather than the group name by putting a hash mark before the GID. User-friendly shells like tcsh lets you enter this directly, while lesser shells such as bash demand you escape the hash mark.

$ **sudo -g \#103 stupidpickycommand**

Sudo now runs the command as if your primary group is 103.

You can combine -u and -g flags, but hopefully your application-specific user is already configured with the optimal primary group.

Changing Usernames but Keeping Your Groups

Running a command as a different user means that you inherit that user's group memberships. It's possible you might need to run a command as a different user, but retain the group memberships associated with your original account. Use the -P flag to change your effective user without changing group memberships. Here **thea** runs a command as **pg**, but retains her original group membership.

```
$ sudo -u pg -P pgsqldump.sh
```

I want to say this is a feature you should never need, but reality is full of server configurations simultaneously horrid and unavoidable.

Viewing Your Sudo Privileges

The second easiest way to figure out your sudo privileges is to blindly run all sorts of commands and see which work and which return errors. Or, you could ask sudo for your privileges by using the -l flag.

```
$ sudo -l
User mike may run the following commands on lucaslaptop:
    (ALL) ALL
```

That's the sudo policy for my account on this host. Now all I have to do is figure out what that means.

Reading Sudoers

Using sudo(8) seems simple because all the real work happens in the sudoers policy. The policy contains the rules dictating which users can run which privileged commands. Unless you're using LDAP or some other policy plug-in, you probably have a literal sudoers file—either */etc/sudoers* or */usr/local/etc/sudoers*. No matter if it's a literal file or handled by the network, "sudoers" represent the policy.

Sudoers contains a series of rules, one rule per line. Every rule uses the same general format. Most of the rest of this book involves somehow extending, stretching, and generally abusing this format.

```
username   host = command
```

The *username* is the user or list of users this rule applies to. The username might also be a system group, or an alias defined earlier within sudoers. Separate multiple usernames with commas.

The *host* is the server or servers this rule applies to. Again, separate multiple hosts with commas. Chapter 10 discusses sharing sudoers across multiple hosts.

The equals sign separates the host from the commands.

Finally, the *command* lists each command this rule applies to. Sudoers requires full paths for all commands. Separate multiple commands with commas.

Sudoers recognizes a variety of special keywords. The most common is ALL, which matches every possible option. To allow all users to run any command on any host, you could write sudoers like so.

```
ALL   ALL = ALL
```

This is roughly equivalent to giving all users root access, but using their own password instead of the root password. Don't do this. At a minimum, restrict access to trusted users.

```
thea   ALL = ALL
```

The user **thea** can run any command on any server that uses this sudoers.

The most common host limitation you'll see is ALL because most sysadmins configure sudo separately on each server. If you manage every server separately, defining the server as ALL really means "this here server." As a best practice, however, put the server's name here.

When your server farm gets large enough that you need to manage sudoers centrally, you'll be very happy you did so. Use hostname(1) to see what the server thinks its name is. Here, **thea** can run all commands on the host **www**.

```
thea    www=ALL
```

To restrict a user to running a single command, give the full path to the command and any arguments.

```
mike    www=/usr/sbin/service apache24
```

The user **mike** can use service(8) to manage the Apache web server on the machine **www**. I'm responsible for the web server and not the operating system, annoying as I find that restriction after decades of sysadmin experience.

This seems perfectly straightforward, right? It is. It really is. Until you start to work in the real world with more than one user or machine.

Multiple Entries

Each unique combination of access rules needs its own sudoers entry. Suppose I get permission to reboot the whole server as well as restart the web service.

```
mike    www=/usr/sbin/service apache24
mike    www=/sbin/reboot
```

This quickly gets cumbersome, especially as I fully intend to pry more access from the system administrator. Combine multiple similar rules by separating the components with commas.

```
mike, pete   www=/usr/sbin/service apache24, /sbin/reboot
```

Users **mike** and **pete** have access to exactly the same commands on the host **www**.

While you can list multiple commands and users in a single rule, you must use different rules for different access levels.

```
thea     ALL=ALL
mike, pete    www=/usr/sbin/service apache24, /sbin/reboot
```

The first rule declares that lead sysadmin Thea can do anything she wants on any server. She has graciously allowed Mike and Pete access to two commands on the host **www**.

Permitting Commands as Other Users

Sudoers assumes users want to run commands as root. You can specify users other than root, however. List the name in parenthesis before the command.

```
kate    beefy = (pg) ALL
```

On the host **beefy**, Kate can run any command so long as she does so as the user **pg**. She can fully manage the database, but has no other special privileges.

Users with access to specific user accounts can also have separate access to root-level privileges.

```
kate    beefy = (pg) ALL
kate    beefy = /sbin/mount, /sbin/umount
```

Kate can run any commands as **pg**, plus she can mount and unmount disks as **root**.

You can combine these entries into one statement.

```
kate    beefy=(pg) ALL, (root) /sbin/mount, /sbin/umount
```

Compactness is not necessarily a virtue in a sudo policy. Use whatever format your most junior coworker can most easily understand.

Special Characters

The sudoers policy reserves some words and characters for internal use. Don't use these within a policy.

The hash mark (#) is the most annoying special character. If it appears in a policy statement in a spot where sudo expects a user ID, and if it's followed by numbers, it's treated as a UID or a GID. The hash mark sets off #include and #includedir statements (Chapter 2). Otherwise, a hash mark is a comment and anything after it is ignored.

Sudo reserves the word *ALL*, in all caps, for internal use. You can't assign a user or host the name ALL. We discuss this built-in alias in Chapter 3.

The exclamation point (*!*) is a negation operator. Negation in sudo isn't as useful as you might hope. Most uses of negation attempt to enumerate badness, which always fails. We discuss negation in Chapters 3 and 4.

Use a backslash (\) to break long rules into multiple lines. Once you list multiple commands by full path, individual sudoers entries can get really long. End a line with a backslash to indicate the rule continues on the next line.

```
kent, mike, pete    beefy,www,dns,mail = /sbin/mount, \
      /sbin/umount, /sbin/reboot, /sbin/fsck
```

Sudoers metacharacters and escape characters are percent signs followed by a letter, such as *%d* and *%H*. The percent sign also denotes groups. Metacharacters and escape characters get used throughout this book.

Whitespace, additional lines, and comments simplify managing sudoers. Use them liberally.

Reading the Policy

Let's look again at the privileges `sudo -l` says I have.

```
User mike may run the following commands on lucaslaptop:
    (ALL) ALL
```

I'm only viewing the privileges for my account (**mike**) on this host (**lucaslaptop**). It gives me the users I can run commands as, and which commands I can run.

As the hostname indicates, this policy is for my laptop. It makes sense that I can run all commands as all users. Once I leave my machine and head into hosts run by the organization I work for, the policy will get much more complex.

Now let's make some policies.

"Now fix your sudoers, or I shall taunt you a second time."

Chapter 2: Managing Sudoers

Sudoers is the core of sudo management. If sudo cannot parse sudoers as a valid policy, it refuses to run. If you rely on sudo to get root privileges and you break sudo, you lock yourself out of privileged commands. Fixing sudoers is a privileged command. Don't do this.

The sudoers file has one inviolate rule, broken only by those who covet misery: *never edit sudoers by hand.* Just as Unix uses vipw(8) and vigr(8) to safely edit `/etc/passwd` and `/etc/group`, sudo provides visudo(8) to safely edit sudoers. Use it.

Visudo locks `/etc/sudoers` so that only one person can edit it at a time. It opens a copy of the file in your text editor. When you save the file, visudo parses it and verifies the sudo grammar. If your new sudoers file is syntactically valid, visudo copies the file back to `/etc/sudoers`. Now you can run sudo, and get a sharp reminder that "syntactically valid" is not the same as "does what you want."

Sudo processes rules in order. If two rules conflict, the last matching rule wins.

While `sudo -l` might strip away a whole bunch of stuff you don't need on a certain host, rule order matters. You'll see examples throughout this book.

A sudoers policy must always end in a blank line. If you see errors complaining about your last line, add a blank line to the end and try again.

Creating Sudoers

While most operating systems include a default sudoers file with many examples, you're here to learn. Learning means making your own sudoers policy from scratch, just like baking a cake but not as delicious. Move the default sudoers file somewhere where you can refer to it, in case it includes OS-specific references. (Apple and Ubuntu users, you *do* have a root password on your learning machine, right?) Become root, and run visudo.

```
# visudo
```

Create a very simple sudoers, giving yourself full privileges to this host. Here Thea gives herself unlimited access.

```
thea    ALL = ALL
```

Save the file and exit. Your text editor should exit and visudo should install our one-rule policy.

Now that you can edit sudoers, let's deliberately break it. (Apple and Ubuntu users, you do have a root password, right?) Run visudo. Pound some keys. Save and exit.

```
/etc/sudoers.tmp: 3 lines, 39 characters.
>>> /etc/sudoers: syntax error near line 2 <<<
>>> /usr/local/etc/sudoers: syntax error near line 3 <<<
```

What now? To throw away your changes, reverting to the previous known-valid policy, enter x. Visudo discards its temporary file and doesn't touch the installed policy. An old working sudoers is better than the new broken one.

If you press e, visudo returns you to the text editor to fix your error. Go to the line specified and figure out what you did wrong. The line numbers are usually correct, unless you've written a multi-line rule. Fix the problem and visudo will let you save the policy.

Press Q and visudo installs your invalid file as the sudoers policy. When sudo cannot parse sudoers, it immediately exits. Pressing Q tells visudo to break sudo until you log in as root and fix it. Do not press this key. It will not improve your life.

If you forget these keys, entering a question mark prompts visudo to print out your options.

Remember that a valid sudoers file is not the same as a useful sudoers file. A blank sudoers, denying all privileges to everyone, is perfectly valid and very quick to parse. I once installed a sudoers file that gave the user `mike` complete access to the host, which was great—except that my username in that organization was `mw18194`. Visudo gleefully accepts sudoers files where every rule specifies users and commands not on the system, or contains only servers other than the local host.

When creating the master sudoers file for an organization, I strongly recommend creating a final rule that gives the senior sysadmin the right to run visudo. If everything else fails, she can fix the rules.

```
thea ALL = /usr/sbin/visudo
```

Always put this rule at the end of the file. Sudo policies are processed in order, and last match wins. Even if an earlier rule forbids running visudo, the senior sysadmin can always recover.

Visudo Editors

Unix editors are powerful management tools. Even the original editor, ed(1), includes shell escapes and other features that render it less of a tool for changing and creating text and more of a chainsaw for sysadmins. As visudo must run with root privileges, allowing use of any editor opens up a bunch of potential security flaws. Visudo defaults to using a single editor—vi(1) on BSD and CentOS, and nano(1) on Debian.

While all sysadmins must have a passing familiarity with vi,[3] that doesn't mean you must perform all tasks with it. The sysadmin can choose which editors she will allow people to use to edit sudoers, however, by setting default editors. We won't talk about sudoers defaults until Chapter 4, but for now nod and smile and go along with it. Set the *editor* variable to the list of permitted editors. Sudo variables go at the top of sudoers. Here's the settings for my laptop.

```
Defaults editor=/bin/ed:/usr/bin/emacs
```

When you run visudo, it tries the listed editors in order. If */bin/ed* exists, visudo uses it. If your ramshackle Unix lacks ed, visudo falls back on */usr/bin/emacs*.

Why would you set multiple default editors? Multiple defaults allow the user to choose which editor to use. Visudo checks the shell environment variable SUDO_EDITOR for a preferred visudo editor, then falls back on VISUAL and, finally, EDITOR.

If you have trouble, search the output of sudo -V for "editor." Skip all the configure options.

```
# sudo -V | grep -i editor
...
Visudo will honor the EDITOR environment variable
Path to the editor for use by visudo: /usr/bin/editor
```

If visudo doesn't explicitly say it will honor EDITOR, it was probably built to ignore it by default. Add the *env_editor* default to tell visudo to accept the user's editor.

```
Defaults env_editor
Defaults env_keep +="SUDO_EDITOR"
```

What's that *env_keep* thing? It lets the user's SUDO_EDITOR survive the transition to root privileges. See Chapter 8.

---

[3] I have very few unbreakable rules for being a "real" sysadmin. One is: real sysadmins can use vi. Vi and ed are the two editors you can be confident of finding on any Unix. "Can't use vi" means "not a real sysadmin." "No ed" means "not a real Unix."

Testing and Verifying Sudoers

Once your sudoers policy grows beyond two lines and starts growing lists and aliases and all those things we'll discuss later, figuring out what a specific user can do grows a bunch more complicated. Additionally, many environments centrally manage their servers and you'll need to be able to validate that the sudoers policy you're pushing to all those machines actually works before you install it. Sudo includes features to test both of these.

User Access Testing

Here's a little drama that plays out every day in every organization. A user or a junior sysadmin requests access to a command, feature, or system. The senior sysadmin makes the requested policy change and closes the request. The junior sysadmin immediately reopens the request and complains that the access doesn't work. If the junior sysadmin has the access and doesn't know how to make it work, that's fine. But if the senior sysadmin didn't properly grant the access, well, if there's one thing sysadmins abhor it's redoing work. It doesn't matter if that work is opening a ticket to get necessary access, or changing the policy change. Everybody's day just got a little bit worse.

Users can list their own sudo privileges by using the -l flag. If you can run sudo as root, you have the ability to view another user's access with the -U flag. Here, senior sysadmin Thea checks my privileges on the host **www1** before closing my ticket.

```
# sudo -U mike -l
User mike may run the following commands on www1:
    (root) /usr/bin/service
```

I have no grounds to complain, much as I'd like to.

If you share a single policy across multiple hosts, you can check a user's access on a host other than the local host with the -h flag.

```
# sudo -l -U pete -h dns9
User pete may run the following commands on dns9:
    (root) ALL
```

Only root and users that can run sudo as root on the current host can use -U. Any user can use -h. My unprivileged user account can only check its own access.

Testing for Automation and Distribution

Lots of folks have Ansible or Puppet or a similar management system, where configuration files are automatically pushed from a central server to all the client servers. These systems are invaluable for maintaining innumerable machines with a minimum of torment. Many of these management systems use sudo to get privileged access to their clients. More than one hapless sysadmin has pushed a non-parsable sudoers or otherwise invalid sudoers across their network, necessitating tedious and exhausting recovery.[4] Avoid such debacles by testing your sudoers policy on the destination machine before installing it.

The -c flag tells visudo to validate a file before installing it. Have your automation system copy the new *sudoers* to a temporary location it controls, test the new sudoer's validity on that host, and install it if and only if it passes. (If you're running an obsolete sudo, using -c might require you to specify the temporary file with the -f flag.)

```
# visudo -c sudoers.new
sudoers: parsed OK
```

If the configuration file does not parse, visudo will give you line numbers of the errors.

The -s flag enables strict checking. Strict checks generate false positives if you have usernames and/or hostnames that contain only capital letters, numbers, and underscores. If you use lower case characters in naming your machines and usernames, enable strict checks.

---

[4] Speaking of distributing catastrophe at gigabit speeds: if you see JP Mens, tell him I said "hi."

Finally, the -q flag silences any output from the validity check. It's useful if your management system will check visudo's return code before installing the new sudoers.

```
# visudo -sqc sudoers.new
# echo $?
1
```

This sudoers is invalid. Don't install it.

Why check the sudoers on the target host, rather than on the management host? The version of sudo on the target host might differ from that on the management host. I've worked for global enterprises running more than two dozen different version of Unix. Some of those hosts needed… help, to put it mildly. Even up-to-date modern Unixes might have different versions of sudo.

If you're curious, check the output of `sudo -V` for the sudoers file grammar version. My Ansible host, on a religiously maintained OpenBSD machine that always has the very latest sudo, uses grammar version 46. My fully up-to-date Debian 9.9 hosts, however, use grammar version 45. The sudoers grammar has been pretty consistent for decades now, and the difference is almost certainly a triviality that affects only a tiny fraction of users. With my luck, I'm in that tiny fraction. So long as my sudoers policy installs and runs correctly on my Debian hosts, I'm good. Validating `sudoers` on the OpenBSD host does *not* guarantee that Debian's older sudo can parse the file.

What if you have a homogenous network? First, you're either lucky or work for a very small organization. Second, don't develop bad habits; a sysadmin who always assumes the worst is the closest thing to happy you'll find in systems administration. Third, unless you continuously redeploy your entire network, some corners and edges of your homogenous network are almost certainly not as homogenous as you think.

Be paranoid; validate.

Including Files in Sudoers

Once you have automation and package management, splitting a configuration file into components feels like the next obvious step. Your organization's custom-built package for the web server software might include a sudo configuration that allows the web management team the access they need. Maybe your organization needs to split your sudoers policy into separate files for management purposes. You can include either specific files or directories.

Including Individual Files

Use an `#include` statement lets you pull a specific file into your sudo policy. Consider the following sudoers.

```
mike    /usr/sbin/service httpd
#include sudoers.sysadmin
thea    ALL=/usr/local/sbin/visudo
```

The first line grants my **mike** account access to service(8) for restarting httpd.

The #include statement in the second line grabs a single file and inserts its contents into exactly this place in the policy. The file *sudoers.sysadmin* is in the same directory as *sudoers*. If you want to include a file from another directory, list it by full path.

Third comes the fail-safe final rule that permits lead sysadmin Thea to run visudo and fix anything that gets busted. Sudo policies are processed in order, and the last match wins.

Be sure to protect your include files exactly as you would *sudoers* itself. My only assigned job responsibility is to manage the web server. But I know I could do a better job running this server if I had greater access, despite the organization's crummy change control and security policies. If I can somehow add a line to the include file, I can leverage that into increased access.

Edit include files with visudo. (Older versions might need `-f` to specify a filename.)

```
# visudo sudoers.sysadmin
```

When you use visudo to edit an included file, it only validates the integrity of that individual file before exiting. To validate your entire policy, run visudo in check mode—preferably with strict checks.

```
# visudo -sc
/usr/local/etc/sudoers: parsed OK
/usr/local/etc/sudoers.sysadmin: parsed OK
```

This confirms that not only is each individual policy file valid, the policy as a whole is coherent.

The `%h` escape character expands to the system's short hostname. You could distribute several policies to all your hosts, but have each host drag in only the policy that applies to itself. The increasing flexibility of management tools has made this approach less common, but you might find it useful in your environment.

```
#include sudoers.%h
```

When you run visudo without giving it a file name, it opens the main *sudoers* and then each include file in turn. For that reason, if you're using include files I recommend keeping the main *sudoers* file as minimal as possible and putting all the actual rules in separate files, giving each its own include statement.

Or, you could just suck in an entire directory of configuration files.

Including Directories

The `#includedir` statement tells sudo to pull in all the files in a directory and assemble them into a sudo policy. It ignores files with a period (.) in the name or that end in a tilde (~), to avoid sucking in temp files from editors. Ponder this sudoers.

```
#includedir /etc/sudoers.d
thea     ALL=/usr/local/sbin/visudo
```

The included files are sucked in, in file order. The sudoers ends with the "Thea can save our skins" fail-safe, in case one of the assimilated files is valid policy language but wrecks system access.

Edit the files in this directory with visudo, exactly as you would individually included files. Again, on older sudos specify the file with -f.

```
# visudo /etc/sudoers.d/11-webmasters
```

This creates the file *11-webmasters* in our sudo directory. Add the rules you want the webmasters to have and exit.

When processing the policy, sudo reads the files in sorted lexical order. You can see how sudo reads files by validating your policy.

```
# visudo -cs
/etc/sudoers: parsed OK
/etc/sudoers.d/00-core: parsed OK
/etc/sudoers.d/01-security: parsed OK
/etc/sudoers.d/1-sysadmins: parsed OK
/etc/sudoers.d/10-audit: parsed OK
/etc/sudoers.d/11-webmasters: parsed OK
/etc/sudoers.d/2-ansible: parsed OK
/etc/sudoers.d/20-logging: parsed OK
/etc/sudoers.d/Detailer-sudoers: parsed OK
/etc/sudoers.d/customers-sudoers: parsed OK
```

The first line shows that our main policy file parses. It then reads each included file, in order. Lexical order resembles alphabetical order more than numerical order. *1* appears after *01*, and *2* comes after *11*. Capital *D* comes before lower case *c*. Your policy statements get processed in this order. The simplest way to avoid sorting problems is to give each file a name starting with a two-digit number: 10, 20, 30, and so on. This gives you room to squeeze other files in between existing files, inserting rules earlier in your policy.

Protect your include directory as you would sudoers itself. If I can insert a file into this directory, I can give myself any privileges I desire.

Now let's look at simplifying sudoers, even as our policies grow more complex.

"Come and see the violence inherent in the sysadmin!"

Chapter 3: Lists and Aliases

Writing a sudoers policy is simple. You just write down who can run what on which machine. What could be easier?

Now repeat that for five hundred users. Make absolutely sure that users with common roles have identical policies. And the folks managing complex applications that run as a specific user? You must include every single command each admin needs access to run as that dedicated user for each and every one of them.

If you had to write all this out in sudoers, you'd just spray-paint the root password on the wall of the break room instead. Fortunately, sudo offers aliases to condense and simplify security policies.

Complicating things further, Unix systems can get information from a whole mess of sources. Some of those sources aren't even vaguely Unixy. If you need a rule that says "All users in the Active Directory group Domain Admins can mount CIFS shares," you can express that in your policy.

Before we get to any of this, let's consider wildcards.

Wildcards

A *wildcard* is a symbol that can match more than one character. Sudo policies lets you use wildcards to match hosts, filesystem paths, and command-line arguments. Sudoers wildcards look a lot like shell or Perl regular expressions, but are based on the operating system's glob(3) and fnmatch(3) functions. Depending on your operating system, these can differ from regular expressions in subtle, infuriating, or inane ways.

Matching Individual Numbers and Characters

The question mark (?) matches any single character. You can use this to apply a rule to everything with a similar name. Suppose you have several Domain Name Service (DNS) servers, each with a hostname like **dns1**, **dns2**, and so on. Your DNS administrator needs complete access to these servers, so you could use the question mark in the host definition.

```
pete    dns?=ALL
```

This sudoers rule applies to hosts **dns0** through **dns9**, but also **dnsQ** and **dns-**.

If you want to match anything within a limited selection of characters, use square brackets. Maybe you want Pete's access restricted to DNS servers 0 through 3.

```
pete    dns[0-3]=ALL
```

You can use any characters within the brackets, such as [a-zA-Z]. You could use [a-zA-Z0-9] to match all letters and numbers. Stack brackets one after another to create longer, specific matches.

```
pete    dns[a-zA-Z][0-9]=ALL
```

User **pete** has unlimited access to host **dnsA9**, but not **dns9**, **dnsA**, or **dnsA99**. Use an asterisk (discussed below) for broader matches.

Be aware that these matches can vary slightly by operating system. I've encountered case-insensitive [a-z] patterns. Don't rely on case in matches.

Sometimes you must match specific characters, rather than a range. You might need to match any of the characters A, c, or h. There's no way to express these as a range, but you can place them in square brackets to match them. Here I permit user to run a program with one of the -A, -c, and -q arguments and no others.

```
pete    ALL=/opt/bin/program -[Acq]
```

Occasionally you need a broader match, though.

Matching Directories

You can write rules that affect all commands in a directory by giving the directory name, ending in a slash. This does not grant access to subdirectories.

```
mike    www1=/bin/, /sbin/, /usr/bin/, /usr/sbin/
```

My account **mike** can run any program in the primary system directories, but not any subdirectories. This grants me access to */bin/cp*, allowing me to copy my own programs into these directories and granting me unrestricted access. Don't do this.

Matching Everything

The asterisk character matches any possible character, with a few exceptions. It matches any number of characters, including zero characters. If Thea permits me to run all programs that start with "a" in a certain directory, she could use a rule like this.

```
mike    www1=/opt/bin/a*
```

I can run any program in */opt/bin* that begins with the letter "a" as root. All I need to do now is figure out how to add a copy of my shell to this directory, give it a name beginning with "a," and I'll gain unrestricted root access! Similarly, watch out when wildcarding access to the directory containing the visudo binary. A user who can run wildcarded programs in */sbin* or */usr/local/sbin* gets visudo access, allowing him to bootstrap his sudo privileges. Not that I would do such a thing.

Combine an asterisk with brackets to match multiple instances of a character. Here, Pete has a policy that allows him to manage any properly named DNS server in your organization; it matches **dns19934** as well as **dns1**.

```
pete    dns[0-9]*=ALL
```

When used for commands, the asterisk does not match the slash character used to separate directories. If you want a user to have access to all the programs in a subdirectory, you must explicitly list that directory.[5]

```
pete    dns1=/usr/bin/*, /usr/bin/X11/*
```

When used for command-line arguments, however, the asterisk does match the slash. A slash, or a space, or anything might be a valid argument to a command.

Wildcard Dangers

Consider this wildcard rule. I asked Thea for the rights to view the system logs.

```
mike    www1=/bin/cat /var/log/messages*
```

I can view the contents of all of the *messages* files. Cool. I might need this when troubleshooting the puny little web server I'm responsible for. Also, I rather enjoy access to view any file on the system, even the encrypted ones locked down by root.

```
$ sudo /bin/cat /var/log/messages /etc/shadow
```

My root access is now assured; it's only a question of time.

---

[5] This example doesn't need the wildcard; listing the directory and ending it in a slash suffices. People keep trying to grant subdirectory access with wildcards, though, so I gotta talk about it.

As the system owner, you must carefully craft wildcard rules. Here's a wildcard that lets user **mike** access all of this host's /var/log/messages files, including the older ones marked with a period and a number, without letting me view all the files on the host.

```
mike ALL=/bin/cat /var/log/messages
mike ALL=/bin/cat /var/log/messages??
```

You could use a range of numbers if you prefer, so long as you explicitly restrict access. Difficult users like myself will exploit any gap you leave us and then claim an absolute lack of malice because that's how Unix works and I just ran my usual commands, don't you know?

In short: only use asterisks if you have no option.

Blocking Everything

Maybe you want to allow a user to run a command, but disallow all arguments. Two double quotes with no space between the matches only the empty string.

```
dirk    ALL=/opt/program ""
```

Dirk can run this program, but only without arguments.

Aliases

A sudoers *alias* is a named list of similar items. Use aliases to refer to a bunch of users, the hosts sudo is run on, the users a command is run as, or a list of commands. Using aliases simplifies policy maintenance. Here's an alias that includes the commands needed to back up and restore Unix systems using the traditional filesystem dump. This contains everything a user needs to manage backup jobs.

```
Cmnd_Alias    BACKUP=/sbin/dump, /sbin/restore, /usr/bin/mt
```

Now that the alias exists, you can use it in a rule to assign your tape monkey the thankless job you'd rather not do yourself.

```
mike            ALL=BACKUP
```

Lucky me.

For one user, an alias might not seem like much of an advantage. If you have several backup operators, however, create an alias that contains all of them. Here I create the TAPEMONKEYS alias for the people who manage backups.

```
User_Alias      TAPEMONKEYS=mike, pete, hank
```

Combining the aliases creates a sudoers rule like this.

```
TAPEMONKEYS     ALL=BACKUP
```

Two alias declarations and one rule replace one much longer rule. You could write the exact same thing without aliases, of course.

```
mike, pete, hank   ALL=/sbin/dump, /sbin/restore, \
/usr/bin/mt
```

This is both longer and more difficult to read. When you add commands or users, it grows even longer. And successful tape monkeys pick up additional duties, lengthening the command list.

Aliases are not just about readability, though. Using aliases make personnel and responsibility changes instantly percolate through sudoers. There's no risk of dozens of cut-and-paste changes numbing your brain.

Alias names can include capital letters, numbers, and underscores, but must always start with a capital letter. CUSTOMERS_2 is a valid alias name, but _CUSTOMERS2 and 2_CUSTOMERS are not. You must define all aliases before using them, so people normally put all aliases at the top of sudoers.

You've already used one alias, the built-in ALL alias. It's really four aliases, one for each type of data you can have a list of. You cannot name your alias ALL; the built-in alias overrides it.

Each alias type exists in a unique namespace. While you can reuse the same names for different alias types. I strongly recommend not doing so.

```
Cmnd_Alias      DB = /db/pg/bin/*, /db/mysql/bin/*
Host_Alias      DB = 192.0.2.0/24
Runas_Alias     DB = pg, mysql
User_Alias      DB = %dba
DB              DB = (DB) DB
```

Your database administrators can run database commands on the hosts on the database network as the database users. We all know what it means. But as your policy grows and these aliases get used elsewhere in the policy, these identical names lead inexorably to confusion, frustration, and a mob at your door.

Now let's consider the four types of data found in sudoers, how to extend them, and how to use them in aliases.

User Lists and Aliases

Every sudo rule starts with a user or list of users. Define a user alias with *User_Alias* and the users that belong in that list.

```
User_Alias          SYSADMINS=thea
User_Alias          GOONS=mike, pete, hank, dirk
```

The user alias SYSADMINS contains one user, **thea**. If our organization gets big enough to pay for another full sysadmin, adding their username to the alias automatically gives them the same access rights as Thea.

The alias GOONS contains four users. When Thea uses this alias in a rule, it affects all four of us lowly goons equally.

This list can take many forms, however. Sudo recognizes usernames from many sources, not just */etc/passwd*. If your organization manages user accounts via LDAP, sudo needs to pull account information from the directory. You might need to pull in information from

Active Directory, or `/etc/group`, or a user alias, or some obtuse system created by three elite techbros in their basement startup and used only by your cutting-edge organization.

Sudo recognizes eight different types of entity you can use as members of user lists. We've seen examples of plain usernames already, so let's talk about the other seven.

Operating System Groups

Sudoers accept operating system groups as defined in `/etc/group`. Give the group name with a percent sign (%) in front of it. You could create the `/etc/group` entry **dba**, add your database administrators to it, and reference it in sudoers.

```
%dba    db*=(pg)ALL
```

Everyone in the **dba** group can run any command as the **pg** user on servers with hostnames beginning with "db."

Some operating systems have a system group for users who can become root or who may use the root password. The default sudoers policy has an example of giving these users unlimited access.

```
%wheel ALL = (ALL) ALL
```

The people in this group don't get any additional access through this rule—members of **wheel** can already use su(1) to become root. But this lets such people acclimate to using sudo.

Remember, use the id(1) command to see what groups your account belongs to.

If your Unix supports users being in many, many groups, you might want to check the *max_groups* and *group_source* options in `sudo.conf` (Chapter 7).

User ID

Use user ID numbers in sudoers by putting a hash mark in front of them.

```
#10000    ALL=/sbin/reboot
```

Any account with UID 10,000 can reboot any machine via sudo. I don't know why you would want this user to run around rebooting everything, but it's not the weirdest configuration I've seen.

If you have multiple accounts with identical user IDs, this rule applies to all of those accounts.

Group ID

If you don't want to use group names, use group ID numbers prefaced by %#. On a traditional Unix system, `wheel` is group 0.

```
%#0    ALL=ALL
```

If the name service that provides usernames is flaky, you might want to try this route to give `wheel` members access. I recommend fixing your name service instead, but you might not control that.

As with user IDs, if you have multiple groups with the same GID, this rule applies to all of them equally.

Netgroup

If you're managing systems via NIS, your next step should be to stop using NIS. Until you reach that point, reference netgroups in sudoers by putting a plus sign before the name.

```
+webmasters ALL=/opt/apache24/bin/*, \
    /opt/apache24/sbin/*
```

Your `webmaster` team can run any command in the two Apache directories.

Using netgroups might require you set the *netgroup_tuple* Default. Older sudo only used the username and domain for user matches. By setting *netgroup_tuple*, you tell sudo to match on the full combination of user, domain, and host.

Non-Unix Group

If your version of sudo has the necessary plugins or patches to support checking against information sources beyond those of traditional Unix systems, you can reference them in sudoers. Preface them with a percent sign and a colon (%:).

```
%:Admins          ALL=ALL
```

Many non-Unix directories use spaces or non-ASCII characters in group names. These characters must be escaped, somehow. Escaping special characters is a pain, so enclose the entire group name (including the leading %:) in double quotes.

```
"%:Domain Admins@internal.mwl.io"    ALL=ALL
```

When in doubt about non-Unix groups, use double quotes.[6]

Non-Unix Group ID

So you've attached your system to a non-Unix directory and you want to use the number of these foreign groups rather than the names? No problem. Put a percent sign, colon, and hash mark (%:#) before the group number.

```
thea,%:#87119301 ACCOUNTING = ALL
```

If you find yourself here, I strongly suggest you step back and reconsider how you're using your directory service.

User Aliases

Your username list can include a user alias.

```
SYSADMINS, fred    loghost?=ALL
```

Both **thea** and **fred** have full control of all hosts with a name beginning with **loghost**.

---

6   Getting emojis in group names to display on your SSH terminal exceeds both the scope of this book and the limits of sanity.

Combine any of these types in a single user list or a single alias.

```
User_Alias    WHINERS mike, +customers
thea, %wheel,"%:Domain Admins",%:#3141529    ALL=ALL
```

These are perfectly valid sudo rules. They're also hints that perhaps your system architect should be repeatedly dipped into the scorpion pit until he sees the error of his ways.

Hosts, Host Lists and Aliases

The hosts portion of a policy rule accepts values other than a list of pure host names. But let's talk about those pure host names first.

Sudo determines the name of the local host by running hostname(1). It ignores any domain name, using only the short name. Sudo does not rely on DNS, */etc/hosts*, LDAP, or any other name directory. The traditional host name `localhost` won't work in a sudoers policy unless that's what hostname returns. (You can change this name with the *fqdn* option, which we'll examine in Chapter 10). This means that the hostname in sudoers must match the hostname on the local machine. If I have console access to the host, I can change the hostname and change the policy that gets applied to the machine. (Anyone with console access has far better and subtler ways to subvert the machine, but still.)

In addition to the local host name, sudoers can accept a variety of IP addresses and netgroups.

IP Addresses

If you use an IP address in a host list, sudo queries all of the local host's interfaces to see if any addresses on them match the rule. Virtual interfaces like bridges and VLANs are queried, but loopback interfaces are not queried. Just like the hostname `localhost`, the addresses 127.0.0.1 and ::1 never match.

Sudo can differentiate between host names and IP addresses, so you don't need to put any special markers in front of an IP address.

```
%dba    203.0.113.207,2001:db8::207=ALL
```

Members of the **dba** group have full control of any machine that has the IP address `203.0.113.207` or `2001:db8::207` attached to it.

You can use networks in sudoers, specifying netmasks in either modern CIDR format (`192.0.2.0/25`) or the obsolete dotted-quad format (`192.0.2.0/255.255.255.128`). If any interface on the machine is in that network, the sudoers rule applies. Here, every server on the network `2001:db8::0/64` is a database development host. Members of the DBA team have full access to these hosts, so that they can figure out what configurations are needed in production.

```
%dba    2001:db8::0/64=ALL
```

If a machine has multiple interfaces on different networks, remember that the sudo policy works on a last-matching-rule basis. If the rules for two networks conflict, the last rule wins.

Netgroups

YP/NIS sites can refer to host netgroups in sudoers by putting a plus sign (+) in front of the name, exactly as you would for an NIS user.

```
carl    +postgres = ALL
```

Most of us will refer to groups of hosts by sudo aliases, however.

Host Aliases

A host alias is a named list of hosts. Indicate a host alias with the string *Host_Alias*. A host alias can include any of the hostname types recognized by sudo. Like user aliases, host alias names must start with a capital letter and may contain capital letters, numbers, and underscores only.

```
Host_Alias    WWW=www*, 2001:db8:3::0/64
```
You can include one host alias inside another.
```
Host_Alias    DMZ=192.0.2.0/24, WWW, BASTION
```
Use the host alias in a rule like so.
```
pete DMZ=ALL
```
Pete now has full privileges on the hosts in the DMZ host alias, including everything defined in the WWW and BASTION host aliases plus a couple of IPv4 and IPv6 networks.

RunAs Lists and Aliases

Grant a user permission to run a command as another user by putting the target username in parenthesis before the command. We saw how to do this earlier.
```
kate    beefy = (pg) ALL
```
Kate can run any command on the host **beefy** as the user **pg**. These are called *RunAs privileges*.

RunAs Lists

Like usernames, RunAs users are lists. Maybe you have multiple database platforms that require separate dedicated users. Your database needs access to run commands on any host as the appropriate database user. Any type of username that's valid in a user list is valid in a RunAs list.
```
%dba ALL=(pg, mysql)ALL
```
Members of the DBA team can run any command on any server, so long as it's run as either **pg** or **mysql**.

You can also let a user run a command as a member of a group, rather than as a specific user. Unix expresses file ownership with a username, a colon, and a group name. To write a rule that permits running a command as a group member, skip the username. Members of the **helpdesk** group are not part of the **operator** group, but the boss wants them to be able to run mksnap_ffs(8) as if they were part of **operator**.[7]

```
%helpdesk ALL=(:operator) /sbin/mksnap_ffs
```

Helpdesk staff now have the power to fill up your hard drives. Congratulations!

RunAs Aliases

You're probably getting the hang of this by now, but let's talk about RunAs aliases anyway. A RunAs alias lets you group users that need to run commands. An obvious choice in our example is a RunAs alias for your dedicated database programs. Use the label *Runas_Alias* to create a RunAs alias.

```
Runas_Alias DB_USERS = pg, mysql
```

Use the string DB_USERS anywhere you'd want to use a list of usernames to run commands as.

```
%dba DB=(DB_USERS)ALL
```

We now have a single, readable rule that lets our DBAs run anything as a database user, so long as they're on a host in the DB alias. If the database team gets broken up into multiple groups, either add the new group to the list or create a user alias to contain all those groups and users.

Command Lists and Aliases

Command lists are the simplest lists in sudo. Unix doesn't store commands in LDAP or NIS; every command exists on a filesystem path. Specify commands by full path, like */sbin/fdisk*, or with a wildcard,

---

7 This is clearly a management decision, as nobody with even minimal technical awareness wants the helpdesk creating UFS filesystem snapshots.

as in /usr/local/bin/*. Put all the desired commands in a comma-separated list.

```
mike    ALL=/sbin/dump, /sbin/restore, /usr/bin/mt
```

There's no way to pull in non-Unix commands. What's on the filesystem is what you've got.

Command Aliases

Command aliases are lists of commands assigned a name and labeled with *Cmnd_Alias*. The rules for naming command aliases are identical to all the other aliases. While all aliases can include other aliases, this feature is perhaps most useful with command aliases.

```
Cmnd_Alias   BACKUP = /sbin/dump, /sbin/restore, /usr/bin/mt
Cmnd_Alias   HELPDESK = /usr/bin/passwd, BACKUP
```

Use a command alias in sudoers anywhere you'd use a command.

Command Tags

A *command tag* is a flag that changes how the command runs. You can use tags before a command list or command alias. We'll cover the ten tags in the appropriate sections of this book, but you should recognize a tag when you see it. A tag appears before the command list, separated from the commands by a colon.

```
mike              ALL=NOEXEC:ALL
```

We'll use this NOEXEC tag in Chapter 5.

Tag names appear in policy statements as all capitals, without any numbers or other symbols. A tag affects all of the commands in the list following the tag.

List multiple tags in one rule by separating them with a colon.

```
thea    ALL = NOPASSWD:EXEC: ALL
```

We cover the NOPASSWD tag in Chapter 13.

Excess Rules

Some policies are more generous than needed. Let's reconsider the database team's privileges.

```
%dba ALL = (pg, mysql) ALL
```

Users in the database group can run any commands as **mysql** or **pg**. They don't need this access on all of the hosts, though. Most database servers run only a single database program. Large organizations have very few systems running both Postgres and MySQL.

In many environments, this extra access doesn't matter. If your DBA attempts to run a command as **pg** on a MySQL server, the command will fail thanks to the user not existing. If the user exists—say, thanks to the wonders of LDAP—the software probably isn't installed and the command will fail. If the software exists but isn't configured, the command will fail. If the DBA attempts to configure MySQL on the Postgres server, well, the sudo logs (Chapter 12) will show who to blame.

On the other hand, giving the DBAs access to shift their hosts from one sort of database to another without bothering you is highly convenient.

Before writing complicated policies, decide how much work you're willing to do to eliminate this extra access. Is the DBA's ability to configure MySQL on the Postgres servers a risk? If so, eliminate that risk.

The Command Alias "ALL" Is Dangerous

The ALL command alias means that the user can run any command with privilege. It's not terrible when you're allowing users to run commands as other users. It doesn't really matter if the database administrator somehow weasels a shell as the database account; they're responsible for that account and that application, and anything that happens is on them to fix. It's fine on your laptop. But in an enterprise where you're looking to restrict access, it's a serious problem.

ALL is useful when combined with RunAs aliases, but giving people access to ALL as root grants them unrestricted root access. If that's your goal, fine. If you're trying to give users restricted access, though, using the ALL command alias grants them root no matter what restrictions you attempt to put on it. Excluding commands does not work. Tags like NOEXEC (Chapter 5) are insufficient. We'll discuss the problems with these in the relevant sections. If you use the command alias ALL in a policy, you grant the user unlimited privilege. Allowing ALL as another unprivileged user, such as the database account, is not terrible. Using ALL when executing commands as root means the user has complete system ownership.

The only secure way to grant users limited access to root privilege is to specifically list what programs they can run. Enumerating badness always fails.

Allowing All Legitimate Commands

You want to grant a user access to every legitimate command. The ALL command alias is unsafe. Granting privileged access to entire directories permits adding commands to those directories, so it's also unsafe. Building a list of every legitimate command is tedious and annoying. It's not like you can download a pregenerated list of all legitimate commands for your hosts; every organization has slightly different Unix installs. You could list whole directories, but then you risk an unscrupulous user adding a shell to `/opt/bin` and rooting your host.

Fortunately, sysadmins have ways to deal with tedious and annoying problems. We script them. Here's a simple Perl script, `createall.pl`, that walks the program directories and lists every program in them.

```perl
#!/usr/bin/env perl

#Create a list of all legitimate commands on the system
#Put list of directories here

@directories = ("/bin", "/sbin", "/usr/bin", "/usr/
sbin", "/usr/local/bin", "/usr/local/sbin");

print "Cmnd_Alias ALLCOMMANDS = ";

foreach $directory (@directories) {

opendir (DIRECTORY, $directory);
   while ( $file = readdir (DIRECTORY)) {
      if($file eq "." || $file eq ".."){ next;}
      print "   $directory/$file, \\ \n";
   }
}
print "   /nonexistent\n";
```

This spills out an alias called ALLCOMMANDS. Direct it to a file.

createall.pl > **/tmp/sudoers.d/10-allcommands**

I put this in a temporary file, so that a lengthy script run or a faulty policy file won't break sudo in production. Copy this to /etc/sudoers.d once you've validated it, as with any other automation. The resulting file contains the list of commands on your host, one per line.

```
Cmnd_Alias ALLCOMMANDS =    /bin/chio, \
   /bin/kill, \
   /bin/pkill, \
   /bin/mv, \
   /bin/rmail, \
   ...
```

Now that you have a list, you can edit it. Create another alias, called BADCOMMANDS. Don't want users executing shells? Add the shells to BADCOMMANDS, and exclude that from the list.

```
Cmnd_Alias BADCOMMANDS=/bin/sh, /bin/bash, /bin/tcsh, \
    /usr/bin/sudo, /usr/bin/sudoedit
%wheel ALL=ALLCOMMANDS, !BADCOMMANDS
```

Maybe the development team needs pretty free access in the dev environment, but should they be running fdisk or parted? A complete list of all commands provides a place to start negotiating actual job roles—also known as "forcing management to do their job."[8]

Negation in Lists

The exclamation point (!) provides *negation*. Use the negation character to exclude items from a list. Negation is very useful for host, user, and RunAs aliases.

```
User_Alias      NOTSCUM = %wheel, !mike
NOTSCUM         test* = ALL
```

The members of the wheel group, with one exception, get full access to hosts with names beginning with "test." Thea says that when I tell her where I put her comfy chair, I might get my access back.[9]

When using the ALL command alias, negation is actively harmful and violently insecure. Never, never, *never* use negation in a command list. Why? Unprivileged users cannot alter their username, or the hostname, or the permissions of other system users. They *can* alter the filesystem. Here's a simple example for why it's bad. Senior sysadmin Thea sets up a command alias for the commands often used to become root, and doesn't let me run any of them.

```
Cmnd_Alias BECOME_ROOT = /bin/sh, /bin/bash, \
    /bin/tcsh, /usr/bin/su
mike    ALL = ALL, !BECOME_ROOT
```

---

8   All those commands you don't recognize? That's the list of man pages you need to read.
9   If I tell the senior sysadmin where I put her comfy chair, I'm never getting access to anything ever again.

So, my account `mike` can run any commands as root except commands that could be used to become root. This seems to work: if I run sudo /bin/sh I'm denied, and I get a nastygram from Thea. Unfortunately for her, I'm as annoying as an obsessed toddler and twice as stubborn.

```
$ cp /bin/sh /tmp/mycommand
$ sudo /tmp/mycommand
Password:
# id
uid=0(root) gid=0(wheel) groups=0(wheel),5(operator)
```

Thea excluded */bin/sh*, but not my copy of the shell that I installed as */tmp/mycommand*. And certainly not the copy of zsh I compiled myself and installed in my home directory.

When building access controls for namespaces that users control, enumerating badness doesn't merely fail: it fails quickly and catastrophically. There is no way to safely or securely exclude commands from ALL. The sudo authors have documented this extensively, have begged people not to do it, and still sysadmins all over the world insist on trying. Nothing screams "I don't read instructions" like using exclusions with the ALL command alias.

You can use exclusions from lists of enumerated commands. Consider the ALLCOMMANDS alias in the previous section, which lists all the binaries and scripts in selected system directories.

```
Cmnd_Alias BECOME_ROOT = /bin/sh, /bin/bash, \
    /bin/tcsh, /usr/bin/su
mike    ALL = ALLCOMMANDS, !BECOME_ROOT
```

Copying */bin/sh* to */tmp/sh* won't give me access, because */tmp/sh* is not in ALLCOMMANDS. I could copy */bin/sh* over a permitted program, but that damages the system and file integrity checks will catch it. It's not evasion—it's outright malfeasance, and the logs would show it.

A proper sudo implementation takes time and care. If you're not prepared to do the work, scale back your ambitions.

Aliases in sudo(8)

A user who checks his privileges with `sudo -l` will see the expanded aliases, not the alias names or their definitions.

```
$ sudo -l
Password:
User mike may run the following commands on www1:
    (root) ALL, !/bin/sh, !/bin/bash, !/bin/tcsh,
!/usr/bin/su
```

I don't see the BECOME_ROOT alias, so I don't know how Thea wrote this policy. The exclamation points do tell me how to get root on this machine, without Thea being any wiser. A sysadmin who doesn't configure sudo correctly certainly isn't reviewing the logs either.

Aliases are a simple way to rationalize and simplify sudoer policies. Now let's change the core of how sudo behaves through options and defaults.

"Your sysadmin was a hamster and your Internet Service Provider smells of elderberries!"

Chapter 4: Options and Defaults

Sudo's standard behaviors accommodate the most common use cases. The interesting thing about the most common use case is how annoyingly uncommon it is. Various options in sudoers can change much of sudo's core behavior. Options can be set as global defaults or attached to specific rules, hosts, users, or commands.

Most options that affect specific sudo functions are discussed in their own chapter. That is, we cover environment-affecting options in Chapter 8 and logging options in Chapter 12. This chapter discussions using options in general, both in association with specific rules and as global defaults.

Defaults

Globally change options with *Defaults* statements. As with the rest of sudoers, Defaults are processed in order. The last Default wins. I'm always torn between "put the Defaults at the top of sudoers so that they're obvious" and "put Defaults at the end so that they aren't accidentally overridden later in the policy." Chapter 3 had one example of Defaults.

```
Defaults editor=/bin/ed:/usr/local/bin/emacs
```

While visudo's usual editor is vi, here we've set the choices to ed and Emacs. You could override this setting in policy statements for individual users, machines, or commands, as we'll see below.

Option Types

Options can be either boolean, integers, strings, or lists or integers usable in boolean context.

Boolean Options

Some options affect sudo merely by being present. They're toggle switches, turning behaviors on and off. Some boolean options are on by default, even when they don't appear in sudoers. Deactivate them by putting them in sudoers, with an exclamation point in front of them.

The classic boolean option is insulting the user.[10] One of sudo's earliest features was to spew an insult when the user mistyped their password. This is now enabled and disabled with an option.

```
Defaults    insults
```

When I type my password incorrectly, I'll receive motivational commentary in addition to a password prompt.

```
$ sudo -l
Password:
I'm very sorry, but I'm not allowed to argue unless
you've paid.
Password:
You speak an infinite deal of nothing
Password:
sudo: 3 incorrect password attempts
```

If your sudo insults users by default, you can disable the insults by disabling the option.

```
Defaults !insults
```

Your users now get the boring password prompt.

---

10   The insults include a variety of Monty Python quotes, which explains but does not excuse this book.

Some operating system packagers deliberately remove this option from their version of sudo. If yours does so, I recommend complaining bitterly until they see the error of their ways.

Integer Options

Some options act as a dial for sudo behavior, letting you turn some features up and down by using a number as an argument. Use an equals sign to separate the argument from the option name. The number sets a limit for the sudo option.

Your users might need more than one attempt to enter their passwords. Proper passwords, with mixed-case letters, numbers, assorted symbols, and DNA samples, aren't easy to type. The *passwd_tries* option lets you set a number of password attempts sudo permits before booting the user and logging an error.

```
Defaults    insults, passwd_tries=5
```

Here we combine two options in one Defaults statement, separated by a comma. While you can use as many options in a single Defaults statement as you want, I recommend grouping options by function.

Integers Usable in a Boolean Context

If an integer option sets a dial for a sudo setting, these options let you disable a feature by setting the limit to zero. Sudo normally caches that you've successfully entered your password for five minutes. The *timestamp_timeout* option lets you change the number of minutes.

```
Defaults    insults, timestamp_timeout=10
```

The longer sudo caches the authentication, however, the greater the risk that the user will walk away from a privileged terminal session. Many users don't lock their workstations when they leave their desk, so using a longer timeout increases the risk of an idle workstation attack.

Avoid idle workstation attacks by disabling authentication caching by setting the timeout to zero. Require the user to enter a password every time they run sudo.

```
Defaults    insults, timestamp_timeout=0
```

Depending on your environment, and what commands people use for sudo, disabling the authentication timer might seem harsh. It can make sense for certain authentication methods, as discussed in Chapter 13.

String Options

Some options need an argument like a text string or a path to a file.

When a user mistypes his password, there's a middle ground between insulting the user and offering the bland "Sorry, try again." Use a custom message by setting the *badpass_message* option. You must disable insults to set a custom message.

```
Defaults         !insults, badpass_message=\
   "Wrong password. Your incompetence has been logged!"
```

I used double quotes because my message has special characters, like whitespace and the exclamation point. Arguments like file paths have no special characters and don't need quotes.

Setting Options for Specific Contexts

Options aren't just global defaults. You can set options so that they affect only certain users, commands, or machines. You must specify each type of default separately.

Per-User Defaults

Certain users need different defaults than others. Perhaps your managers need different authentication timeouts or a different password prompt. Maybe some whiner who should have never been given an account complained that the system insulted him. Change the defaults for specific users by using the *Defaults* keyword, a colon, the user list or alias, a space, and the option.

The first time you run sudo on any machine, it prints a short lecture reminding you to be careful. Most users need that reminder. System administrators are continuously mindful of their responsibilities and are painfully aware of the damage they can do with a misplaced keystroke.[11] They don't need reminding, and once they've seen the lecture hundreds of times it only annoys them. Here Thea disables the *lecture* option for herself.

```
Defaults:thea    !lecture
```

She could also disable the lecture for everyone in the **wheel** group, affecting those folks permitted to use the root password.

```
Defaults:%wheel    !lecture
```

The people who have root privileges will now be very slightly less annoyed.

Per-Host Defaults

To override sudoers defaults on a per-host basis use Defaults, an at symbol (@), the host list or alias, and then the option.

```
Defaults      lecture
Defaults@TESTHOSTS    !lecture
Defaults@PRODUCTION   lecture=always
```

The first rule establishes the default of lecturing the user once per machine.

The second rule disables lectures on hosts in the TESTHOSTS alias. It's the test environment, the right place to make your horrific but educational mistakes.

The third rule sets the *lecture* option to "always" for all hosts in the PRODUCTION alias. This shows the lecture every time the user must

---

11   I said that with a straight face? Wow.

enter their password, not necessarily every time the user runs sudo. Remember, sudo caches successful authentication for five minutes.

It's the last rule, so it overrides all previous rules. This means that if a host appears in both the TESTHOSTS and PRODUCTION aliases, the PRODUCTION rules apply. (Having hosts classified as both "test" and "production" is an administrative nightmare, but sudo doesn't care.)

Per-Command Defaults

To set per-command or command alias defaults use *Defaults*, an exclamation point, and the command list or alias, then the options.

Perhaps some users can be trusted, most of the time. But maybe a specific user has difficulty with a particular command. Or maybe a certain problem has happened once too often.

```
Cmnd_Alias          PARTITIONERS=/sbin/fdisk, /sbin/gpart
Defaults!PARTITIONERS lecture=always, \
    lecture_file=/etc/fdisk-lecture
```

The *lecture_file* option lets the sysadmin write a custom lecture message in a text file. In this case, `/etc/fdisk-lecture` contains a lecture specifically to be used for the disk partitioning tools gpart(8) and fdisk(8).

```
If you repartition an important disk again, Thea will
leave the tatters of your still-living body in the break
room as a warning to others.
```

The lecture appears only if the user must authenticate. To have the lecture appear every time this rule is hit, require the user to enter a password every time by setting *timestamp_timeout* to 0.

```
Defaults!PARTITIONERS lecture=always, \
    lecture_file=/etc/fdisk-lecture, timestamp_timeout=0
```

With this configuration, every time I try to partition a disk I view Thea's threat—er, *lecture*—and must enter my password.

You can use a command list instead of an alias. I find this less readable and less maintainable.

```
Defaults!/sbin/fdisk, /sbin/gpart lecture=always
```

Command tags can be defaults.

```
Defaults!ALL    NOEXEC
```

This default sets the NOEXEC tag any command accessed through the ALL command alias.

Per RunAs Defaults

To set a default for a RunAs rule, use a right angle bracket between *Defaults* and the user list.

```
Defaults>operator     lecture
```

Anyone who runs a command as **operator** gets lectured when they get a password prompt.

Conflicting Defaults

Consider the following sudoers policy.

```
Defaults:mike    insults
Defaults!/usr/bin/su    !insults
mike    ALL=/usr/bin/su
```

The first line says to insult me every time I run sudo. The second line says that whenever someone runs su via sudo, don't insult them. The third line gives me the right to run su. The defaults conflict. What happens?

```
% sudo su - root
Password:
Sorry, try again.
```

Sudo does not insult me.

Remember, sudoers policies work on a last match basis. The last matching Default statement says "don't insult su users." To insult me, reverse the order of the two Defaults statements—or, just put a general "insult the problem user" rule at the bottom of the policy.

Options and Lists

Some options contain lists that you might need to add entries to, or remove entries from. The most commonly seen is *env_keep*, discussed in Chapter 8. The *env_keep* option contains a list of environment variables. Certain policies might need to add or remove variables from this list.

Use += to add entries to any existing list.

```
env_keep += "FTP_PROXY HTTP_PROXY"
```

This adds FTP_PROXY and HTTP_PROXY to any existing list.

```
env_keep -= "HOME"
```

You can't combine += and -= statements in one policy line. They need to be separate. Chapter 8 has many examples of adding and subtracting from lists.

We'll play with options and defaults for the rest of this book.

> *"All right, but apart from the patches, the package installations, the hardware management, the storage expansion, the upgrades, the backups, the log analysis, and the resource allocation, what has the sysadmin ever done for us?"*

Chapter 5: Shell Escapes, Editing, and Policies

Unix software grows new features like the Pacific Northwest grows moss. They're everywhere. One popular feature is the shell escape, which lets users run commands from within a program. Everything from vi to less(1) and more(1) has shell escapes. Even the primordial ed editor included shell escapes. They're a core expectation in Unix.

If you've never used a shell escape, try it now. View a file with more(1). While you're still viewing the file, enter an exclamation point and a command like `ls` or `ifconfig`. The command will run, displaying the output, and then return you to your `more` session. Once you play with shell escapes for a while, you'll wonder how you endured without them.

Sysadmins who worked with line printers, dumb terminals, and even SLIP connections desperately needed shell escapes. You didn't want to leave a file just to verify if the IP address on your machine matched something in the file. Now that we can have umpteen SSH sessions from our cellphones to a single server, shell escapes aren't so vital.

Unless you use sudo. Then shell escapes become really amazing, in a bad way. Consider the following sudoers policy.

```
mike    ALL=/usr/bin/less
```

I can use `less` to view any file on any host. That's cool. I can look at, say, secure logs to see why a user's SSH connections fail. But I'm running `less` as root. This means any commands that I can execute using the pager's shell escape runs with root privileges. If I run `sudo less /var/log/secure` and then enter:

`!visudo`

I'm in the sudo policy editor. I can edit the policy as I like, save, and exit. Visudo will install the new policy and return me to the `more` session. Now I check my privileges.

```
% sudo -l
User mike may run the following commands on www1:
    (root) /usr/bin/more
    (root) ALL
```

If the senior sysadmin discovers this, she'll want my head on a platter.

When a user has access to a limited subset of privileged commands, you must ensure that he cannot bootstrap himself into greater access. Do this either through permitting only commands that have no shell escapes, or by prohibiting commands from executing other commands. Verifying that a program has no shell escapes is very hard. I'd like to recommend reading the program manual page but I can't—not all documentation is truly complete. The only real test is auditing the source code to every program and library. The only *realistic* solution is to prevent programs from spawning other programs.

Forbidding Commands from Executing Commands

Shell escapes aren't the only way to escape a program. Many programs run other programs. We've already looked at visudo, which runs a text editor. Programs like Sendmail and Nagios function by spawning other processes. I could make a list but, again, enumerating badness always fails. You're better off telling sudo to block all attempts to spawn another process, and then listing what you need.

Sudo uses the LD_LIBRARY_PRELOAD or LD_PRELOAD environment variables to disable programs executing other programs. All modern Unixes support this function, but check your operating system documentation if you're unsure about yours.

The EXEC and NOEXEC tags and options control whether a command may execute commands. EXEC, the unwritten default, allows commands run under sudo to run their own commands. NOEXEC forbids execution, and is also available as the *noexec* option. Put the tag before the command in your sudoers rule.

```
mike    ALL=NOEXEC: /usr/bin/less
```

Now use `sudo less` to examine a file, and try a shell escape into visudo or even a command prompt. Instead of your command executing, `less` prints a message like "done" or "exec failed." It tried to run the command, and failed.

You can't just slap NOEXEC on globally, however. Consider this policy.

```
%wheel    ALL=NOEXEC: ALL
```

People who can become root can run any command, but can't run commands via that command. Some commands must run other commands, though:

```
% sudo visudo
visudo: unable to run /bin/emacs: Permission denied
visudo: /etc/sudoers.tmp unchanged
```

Visudo needs to run a text editor. I can't become root via sudo to fix this, because */bin/sh* must also start processes to be particularly useful. I recommend using a global block, then watching your workload to see what commands legitimately run other commands.

We know that visudo needs to run a text editor. On my mail server, I quickly learned that newaliases(8) legitimately needs to run `sendmail`. A very savvy intruder might perhaps get newaliases to spawn a privileged shell, but that attack considerably raises the skill needed to penetrate your host.

I recommend setting *noexec* as a default, and using a command alias to create a list of commands that may execute commands.

```
Defaults    noexec
Cmnd_Alias  MAYEXEC = /usr/bin/newaliases, /sbin/visudo
%wheel    ALL = EXEC: MAYEXEC
```

The first rule establishes that the default is NOEXEC. The alias MAYEXEC lists programs that must be able to run other processes. The third statement allows users in **wheel** to run the programs in MAYEXEC. A user might have permission to run sudo `/bin/sh`, but that new shell won't be able to execute any commands other than those built into the shell.[12] The user could still damage the system, but doing so demands greater expertise.

Many third-party sudo tutorials recommend forbidding specific programs from executing other programs, much as they suggest excluding commands. Both cases suffer from the same problem: a malicious user can copy programs elsewhere on the disk, changing the policy that applies to the binary. Enumerating badness always fails.

Remember that NOEXEC works through a shared library. This means it has no effect on a static binary. Can your users compile or install their own shell as a static binary? Does your operating system ship with any shells as static binaries? (FreeBSD, notably, ships with a static `/rescue/sh`.) If they can, allowing the user the ability to run those with sudo means they have root access.

---

12 Running a shell that can't execute programs is an education. Try it sometime.

Allowing the user to run any binary with privilege gives the user that privilege, no matter what restrictions you place on it. Create a script to list only the permitted programs, as shown in Chapter 3.

Removing a program's ability to execute other programs still leaves obscure gaps, though. Many programs spawn pagers like less(1), which have all sorts of weird features guaranteed to vex a sudo administrator. We'll cope with pagers in Chapter 8.

That still leaves us with the problem of editors, though.

Editing Files

The reason text editors still have shell escapes is because they're so danged useful. As a user, I might need access to edit a file that's critical for my job. The sysadmin might try a policy like this to give me that access.

```
mike ALL = NOEXEC: /usr/bin/vi /etc/httpd.conf
```

This would give me the ability to edit the file without shell escapes, sure. But it has more general problems. First, it involves the sysadmin in editor wars. I can guarantee you that a substantial portion of users will dislike whatever editor you permit them. I might have a legitimate need for a shell escape while editing this file. Finally, the user must run this exact command. Running `cd /etc/ && sudo vi httpd.conf` won't match.

Here's where *sudoedit* comes in.

Sudoedit(1) lets a user edit a privileged file without running an editor as root. When you run sudoedit on a file, sudo copies the target file to a temporary file, sets the permissions on that file so that you can edit it, and runs your editor on it. You edit the file with your usual, unprivileged text editor. When you exit the editor sudoedit inspects the temporary file. If the file has changed, sudoedit copies it to the target file. Sudoedit lets users have their shell escapes and other fancy editor features without worrying about privilege.

Configuring Sudoedit

To configure editing permissions, use the *sudoedit* keyword and the full path to the target file.

```
mike    www* = sudoedit /etc/httpd.conf
```

I can now edit the web server configuration via sudoedit.

Don't give the full path to the sudoedit command; you're granting the sudoedit privilege in this rule, not rights to run sudoedit(8) as root. Do not grant users permission to run `sudo sudoedit`. This grants the right to edit files using a text editor running as root, also known as "unrestricted privileged access."

Using Sudoedit

To edit a file, run sudoedit(1) and the file name.

```
$ sudoedit httpd.conf
```

Sudoedit checks the user's environment for SUDO_EDITOR, VISUAL, and EDITOR, in that order. If those don't exist, it checks for an *editor* setting in the policy. If none of these exist it falls back on sudo's default editor, as discussed in Chapter 2.

Sudoedit opens the temporary copy of the file in the chosen editor. You can use your editor normally, including shell escapes. Once you save and exit, sudoedit copies the changed file over the original.

Symlinks and Directory Ownership

Symlinks open all sorts of opportunity for mischief. If a user can create a symlink to a file, then edit that symlink, they've edited the actual file. Sudoedit won't open symlinks by default. Enable following symlinks by setting the *sudoedit_follow* option.

Allow sudoedit to follow symlink for particular files by using the FOLLOW command tag. One use might be for the mail aliases file you'll find in */etc/aliases*, which is often a historical compatibility symlink to some other file.

```
mike ALL=FOLLOW: sudoedit /etc/aliases
```

Your policy can override an earlier FOLLOW tag with NOFOLLOW.

Similarly, if a user can write to a directory they can trigger all sorts of mayhem. By default, sudoedit refuses to edit a file in a directory the user can write in. It also checks for writable parent directories and symlinked parent directories, and refuse to run if it finds any. Disable these checks by turning off the *sudoedit_checkdir* option.

```
Defaults !sudoedit_checkdir
```

These directory checks are not applied to **root**.

Policies and Commands

You now have all the pieces that make up a sudoers policy. Everything else builds on these first chapters. Building a policy is not about the individual statements, but how you assemble them into a whole.

Chapter 3 demonstrates how excluding commands lets people run arbitrary commands as root. This chapter shows how shell escapes give people root. While sudo logs all commands by default, it doesn't necessarily log everything that those commands do. Programs like sudoreplay(8) (Chapter 12) give more detailed output, but require configuration.

The natural question is: what good are the sudo tools if a user can ignore restrictions so easily? Part of this problem comes from Unix's complexity and power, true, but never blame your tools.

If your users can run arbitrary commands as root, it's because you wrote a bad policy.

Don't be too embarrassed—the overwhelming majority of people write poor sudoers policy. Many Unixes ship with a policy that permits all users in an administrative group unlimited access. This policy means that your administrative users can do anything, without even being logged. A malicious user or intruder can do an awful lot of damage behind a shell escape.

So, what to do?

The only way to write a secure sudoers policy is to deny commands by default. Use of the ALL command alias gives people too many ways to gain unlimited access. Users will work furiously to get around restrictions that they believe block them from doing their work. Don't leave them a hole to squirm through; instead, use your policy to insist that such problems be solved at the administrative level.

Consider your sudoers policy like a firewall. Back in the 10baseT era, people ran firewalls that permitted all access and then blocked traffic to vulnerable services. On today's Internet, that's a sign of incompetence. Treat your sudoers policy the same way. Default permit sudoers rules make me proclaim "The 90s called, they'd like their security policy back."

The mere presence of the word ALL in the command portion of a sudoers rule means that the user can get unrestricted root access regardless of any restrictions you might think you've placed on him. You cannot enumerate badness in a sudoers policy any more than on a firewall; the only safe practice is to permit only known necessary activity. From this point on, we never use the ALL command alias except to specifically illustrate poor practice. To do otherwise is to invite abuse and intrusion.

You can safely use the ALL alias for user, Run As, and host lists. Unprivileged users cannot change usernames or hostnames.

Another common policy mistake is to let users execute commands in a directory that they own. Maybe `/home/mike/bin` has a bunch of useful stuff in it right now. But the moment you let **mike** run a command with privilege in that directory, he'll put a copy of `/bin/sh` in there. Only permit sudo access to commands in directories completely controlled by root.

It's one thing to not be embarrassed by errors when learning, but you now know better. Do better.

We'll talk more about complicated policies in Chapter 10. For now, let's configure sudo.

"My sudo is full of eels."

Chapter 7: Configuring Sudo

Wait just a dang minute! Isn't this whole book about configuring sudo? What have we been reading about, anyway?

We've been configuring sudo security policies in sudoers, and testing policy with the sudo(8) command line. Here we discuss the behavior of the sudo binary, and how to change core sudo functionality in `sudo.conf`.

Sudo's Default Configuration

The sudo software suite as downloaded from https://sudo.ws ships with a default configuration, but your operating system packager has probably changed some of those settings. Identify the actual defaults of your local install by using sudo's -V flag. Running this as an unprivileged user displays the sudo version and the revision of various syntax and grammar parsers.

```
$ sudo -V
Sudo version 1.8.27
Sudoers policy plugin version 1.8.27
Sudoers file grammar version 46
Sudoers I/O plugin version 1.8.27
```

Running the exact same command as **root** tells sudo to spill its guts for over a hundred lines.

```
# sudo -V
Sudo version 1.8.27
Configure options: --sysconfdir=/usr/local/etc --with-
ignore-dot --with-tty-tickets --with-env-editor
--with-logincap --with-long-otp-prompt
…
Sudoers policy plugin version 1.8.27
Sudoers file grammar version 46

Sudoers path: /usr/local/etc/sudoers
Authentication methods: 'pam'
…
Follow symbolic links when editing files with sudoedit
…
```

The configure options might be irrelevant for you, but the later entries show key facts like "where to look for `sudoers`" and how sudo authenticates. Some default behavior doesn't show up in the output. Sudo ignores symlinks by default, so it only prints out the message about following symlinks when you've enabled *sudoedit_follow*. You'll see lists of environment variables that are retained by default and those that get purged, as discussed in Chapter 8.

Some of these settings are hard-coded into sudo. You can't enable insults or PAM if the binary wasn't built with that support. Other settings can be changed in `sudo.conf`.

sudo.conf

Configure the sudo binary in the optional configuration file `sudo.conf`. Depending on your system and how you installed sudo, you'll find `sudo.conf` in `/etc/` or `/usr/local/etc/`. The file might not exist, as sudo normally runs just fine without any configuration, but your Unix should install a sample file somewhere. Most functions configured in `sudo.conf` are not intended for broad usage. If you read the manual you'll find solutions for problems like "sudo is slow on hosts with unspeakably large numbers of virtual interfaces" or "my install uses an unusually large number of groups that exceeds the built-in defaults"—real problems that affect only a tiny fraction of people. The solutions are vital if you're in that tiny fraction, but not common enough that I need explain every one of them in this book. My goal is to explain the syntax using the more common cases, so that when you need to configure one of these solutions you know how they work.

The `sudo.conf` file has four basic configuration types: Path, Plugin, Set, and Debug. Chapter 12 discusses Debug as part of logging, but we'll touch on the others here.

Path gives a filesystem path where sudo should look for supporting binaries, programs, and other information for specific sudo functions. If you make multiple Path entries for one keyword, sudo uses only the last. Disable a Path by leaving the path blank. We'll discuss Path further in "Plugins" later this chapter.

```
Path plugin_dir /usr/local/libexec/sudo/
```

Sudo's policy processing and I/O functions are modular, and you can replace them with plugins that change sudo's behavior. *Plugin* tells sudo where to find these plugins.

```
Plugin sudoers_policy sudoers.so
```

Set enables and disables features inside the sudo binary, as discussed in "Core Dumps" below. Each feature has a keyword, and can be set to *true* or *false*.

```
Set probe_interfaces false
```

We'll illustrate these parameters by discussing core dumps and plugins.

Sudo Core Dumps

Sudo handles security-sensitive information. It normally keeps that information in wired memory, and discards it as soon as possible. It's also a setuid program, and setuid programs are tempting targets for intruders. For these reasons, sudo doesn't even try to produce a core dump after a crash.

If sudo crashes when you try to run it, though, you might need core dumps to solve the problem. Enable coredumps by setting *disable_coredump* to false.

```
Set disable_coredump false
```

Sudo will now attempt to write a core file, but most operating systems don't allow setuid/setgid programs to dump core. Most Unixes have a sysctl toggle to permit these programs to dump core. Enable core dumps on FreeBSD by setting *kern.sugid_coredump* to 1. On OpenBSD, setting *kern.nosuidcoredump* to 0 dumps core in the current directory, 2 dumps core in /var/crash, and 3 in a subdirectory of /var/crash named after the program. On Linux, set *fs.suid_dumpable* to 2.

Plugins

A sudo plugin replaces either the policy engine or the input/output system, altering sudo's behavior in a fundamental way. The policy engine that reads sudoers is a plugin. If you want to use an alternate logging or input system, use an I/O plugin.

For many users, plugins are an esoteric topic. I debated including them in this book, but you must comprehend plugins to change the location of the sudoers file, so here they are. Using a sudo plugin requires figuring out where you're going to put the plugin, and telling sudo about that plugin.

Plugin Path

Sudo plugins are implemented as shared libraries. The parameter *plugin_dir* tells sudo where to look for plugin libraries. Sudo defaults to using `/usr/local/libexec/sudo` as the plugin directory, but Linux distributions tend to stick it elsewhere.

If you're using a bunch of plugins, want them all in one directory, and don't want to tamper with package-managed directories, you might set a custom plugin_dir.

```
Path plugin_dir /opt/libexec/sudo
```

Others will find it easier to copy the plugin libraries into their sudo's default plugin_dir and ignore complaints from their package manager.

Installing Plugins

Two plugins exist right now: the commercial Privilege Manager for Sudo from One Identity, and the freely available sudo_pair from Square. Check the sudo web site https://sudo.ws for the current list. We'll use sudo_pair as an example.

Sudo_pair (https://github.com/square/sudo_pair) is an I/O plugin that requires a second human being to monitor and approve sudo commands before sudo will execute the command. A user who wants to run a privileged command must find another user to watch their work and approve the change. Both the user and the approver are on the hook for any problems. It's not useful for a lot of small shops, but if your IT department is bound by federal regulations and subject to contractual fines for each minute of downtime, having another human being double-check your work is invaluable.

Each plugin is available as a shared library. The plugin has a name, hard-coded in that library.

To enable a plugin in `sudo.conf` give the Plugin keyword, the name of the plugin, and the path to the plugin's dynamic library. If the library is in the directory with the rest of your sudo plugins (`/usr/local/libexec/sudo` by default), you don't need to use a full path. Otherwise, give the full path. Put any arguments after the shared library name.

```
Plugin sudo_pair sudo_pair.so binary_path=/usr/scripts/pair_approve
```

Sudo can support any number of I/O plugins, but sudo can only use one policy engine at a time. Competing policy enforcement engines is a disaster that won't wait to happen.

Configuring the Sudoers Policy

Sudo knows the default location for the `sudoers` policy file—you see it when running `sudo -V` as root. Some environments need to set a different location for that policy, or need unusual permissions on the file. Set all of these as arguments to the sudoers plugin.

```
Plugins sudoers_policy sudoers.so sudoers_file=/etc/sudoers.mycorp
```

Set the path to the sudoers policy with the *sudoers_file* argument. Change the file's owner with *sudoers_uid* and the group owner with *sudoers_gid*. Both of these must be specified numerically.

The `sudoers` file is normally readable by the owner and the group. Change the permissions with the *sudoers_mode* argument. Give the permission as octal. Here, I make `sudoers` readable only by the file owner.

```
Plugin sudoers_policy sudoers.so sudoers_mode=400
```

Users in the file's group can now only view permissions shown by `sudo -l`.

When you can manage core dumps and plugins, you should have no trouble making further tweaks to the sudo binary.

> *"What is the chair-speed velocity of an unladen sysadmin?"*
> *"Linux or BSD?"*
> *"I don't know that—AAAAAAGH!"*

Chapter 8: Environments

A user's shell environment might not be conducive to good system management. Environment variables exist to alter software behavior. Software running with elevated privileges needs to behave well, and environment variables that change that behavior can threaten the system. Sudo therefore removes most of the user's environment before running the command.

If you've never really considered your environment, run env(1). You'll see some familiar items in there, such as SHELL and PATH, but will also find a bunch of less well-known variables like SHLVL or G_BROKEN_FILENAMES or EDOOFUS or whatever. Some of these are important to you as a user. Some were put in place to work around bugs in notably boneheaded software. Many linger on from prior aeons of systems administration and need to join line printers and SLIP in the Great Digital Boneyard. Purging the environment helps ensure that privileged commands run as expected.

Sudo-Specific Environment Variables

Before cleaning up your environment, sudo injects its own variables into the environment of every command you run: SUDO_COMMAND, SUDO_USER, SUDO_UID, and SUDO_GID. The SUDO_COMMAND variable contains the exact command you ran via sudo to start this session. SUDO_USER gives the original username. SUDO_UID and SUDO_GID give your original UID and primary GID.

A program or script can check for the presence of these variables and utilize them if present. You could use SUDO_USER in log messages, for example. "Yes, I was run by root, but really I was run by `mike`. Blame him."

These are a convenience. Other environment variables, less so.

Dangerous Environment Variables

How can environment variables be dangerous? Programs get their settings from environment variables. Shells use HOME to identify the user's home directory and VISUAL to pick which editor to fire up. These are pretty safe.

But some programs accept LD_LIBRARY_PRELOAD to identify directories that contain shared libraries that should be loaded before the main system libraries. It's a feature intended to support an unprivileged user running personal software, but that directory might contain a modified libc that copies your authentication credentials to a remote server. Different Unixes have a whole family of LD_ environment variables. Shells like Bash use IFS to give the character that separates command-line arguments. Changing IFS to a carefully chosen value can make commands throw a tantrum. Changes to HTTP_PROXY or PATH can trigger catastrophe. I lost an hour writing Chapter 5 because I had somehow set EDITOR to */bin/sh*.

Losing your browser bookmarks because of an incorrect environment variable is vexing. Trashing a server because of an environment variable is worse.

Programs control which environment variables they check for. Commercial software often uses hundreds of environment variables to store arbitrary configurations, much as Microsoft Windows uses the Registry. Variables that are safe on one system can devastate another, so there is no master list of dangerous environment variables.

Sudo lets you control which shell environment settings are passed from the user's environment through to privileged commands.

Execution Environment

Sudo doesn't just run a privileged command for you. It spins up an instance of a shell, runs the command, exits the shell, and returns command to your original shell. This is why commands like `sudo cd /opt/secret/` don't work as you might expect. Sudo starts a shell, changes that shell to that directory, and exits the shell. Your running shell is still where it was before, while the shell instance in the desired directory no longer exists.

You want to see what's in the secret directory? Try `sudo ls /opt/secret/`. You want to run a more complicated series of shell commands? Explicitly start a shell instance and write your commands as a quoted string.

```
$ sudo sh -c "cd /opt/secret ; du -d1 | sort -rnk 1"
```

Here I start a shell instance, gather the total size of all directories in the secret directory, and sort them by size, largest first. The exact specifics of the shell command don't matter; the point is that I had sudo run a list of shell commands via `sh -c`.[13]

The new shell has a minimal environment, with the TERM, PATH, HOME, MAIL, and SHELL settings from the target user. Sudo then injects the special SUDO_ environment variables discussed earlier. If either USER or LOGNAME is set in the original user's environment, they're both set to the target user's username. Sudo then allows the target shell to inherit certain environment variables and filter out others.

---

13   Yes, running a shell requires privileges to run a shell.

Environment Variable Filtering

As root, run `sudo -V`. Near the bottom you'll see lists of environment variables to sanity-check, unilaterally remove, and preserve. These lists are a combination of defaults settings and sudoers options.

Preserving Environment Variables

Sudo keeps a list of environment variables that will be passed from the user's environment to the target environment, shown as "Environment variables to preserve." The default list is COLORS, DISPLAY, HOSTNAME, KRB5CCNAME, LS_COLORS, PATH, PS1, PS2, XAUTHORITY, and XAUTHORIZATION.

These are sensible for most environments. There's no harm in retaining colors in a privileged terminal. If you're using X or Kerberos, you want them to keep working. Retaining your shell prompts is also fairly harmless. The most dubious is PATH. You can impose a new PATH as discussed later this chapter.

Alter this list with the *env_keep* option. Use the += option to add to the list, and -= to remove from the list. A plain equals sign overwrites the entire list. Then put either a single environment variable, or double-quote a list of variables. For example, native Russian speakers probably want commands that run under sudo to retain their preferred character set.

```
Defaults env_keep += \
    "LANG LANGUAGE LINGUAS LC_* _XKB_CHARSET"
```

Perhaps your users need to retain their SSH environment variables, so they can copy files across the network securely.

```
Defaults env_keep += \
    "SSH_CLIENT SSH_CONNECTION SSH_TTY SSH_AUTH_SOCK"
```

You could shorten the SSH policy, if you trust the user to not put silly things beginning with SSH_ in their environment.

```
Defaults env_keep += "SSH_*"
```

Or maybe you just can't trust the user' PATH, and want to use the target user's settings.

```
Defaults env_keep -= PATH
```

While sudo normally strips all Bash functions from the environment, you can permit them by name. You must include the equals sign and parenthesis. Here I allow the Bash function "petulance."

```
env_keep += "BASH_FUNC_petulance%%=()*"
```

Retain all Bash functions by using wildcards.

```
Defaults env_keep += "*=()*"
```

This isn't the complete list of environment variables that get preserved, though. Some variables are sanity-checked and then passed through.

Sanitizing Environment Variables

Certain environment variables can trigger bad behavior if they contain percent signs (%) or slashes (/). Sudo tests these variables for these characters. If the bad characters are present, the environment variable is dropped. Otherwise, it is passed. The environment variables COLORTERM, LANG, LANGUAGE, LC_*, LINGUAS, TERM are automatically checked.

Sudo uses a longer list of checks to validate the TZ environment variable. Clever people have performed all sorts of chicanery with TZ, and sudo guards against everything we know about.

Adjust the list of environment variables to be sanity-checked with the *env_check* option. Don't sanity check all environment variables; many legitimately contain percent signs and slashes.

Suppose some fiend figures out how to attack systems by setting the environment variable COLORS to a filesystem path. The *env_check* option tests for slashes (and percent signs) in variables. You'd need to remove it from the list of environment variables to unilaterally pass through, and add it to the list of variables to sanity check.

```
Defaults env_keep -= COLORS
Defaults env_check += COLORS
```

Privileged commands run via sudo are now protected from this attack.

If a variable is listed in both *env_keep* and *env_check*, *env_check* has priority. If *env_check* rejects an environment variable, it does not get passed even if it's also listed in *env_keep*.

These two lists combine to form sudo's standard shell environment.

Sudo's Standard Shell Environment

Now that we've discussed how the various lists work, let's see how they work together to create the sudo shell environment.

A sudo session is reset to a minimal environment, containing only TERM, PATH, HOME, MAIL, and SHELL. If LOGNAME and/or USER are set in the original user's environment, both get set to the target user.

Sudo applies its list of environment variables to sanity check. Environment variables that pass the sanity check get inserted into the user's environment. Alter the list with the *env_check* option.

Any preserved environment variables are then applied, so long as nothing on the list was blocked by sanity checking. Change the list of preserved settings with the *env_keep* option.

Sudo then injects its own SUDO_ environment variables.

Once the environment is fully configured, the command runs.

Keep Nothing

Perhaps you want the user to retain nothing of their environment. They need a stripped-down minimal environment and that's it. Disable *env_keep* and *env_check* to remove those features.

```
Defaults !env_keep
Defaults !env_check
```

The user now gets a minimal environment, with a handful of environment variables, and that's it.

Setting the Environment for One Rule

You can attach *env_keep* and *env_check* to specific users, machines, commands, and RunAs lists. This lets you tune sudo to better fit specific situations.

Suppose you want to permit use of scp(1) to copy files between hosts, but don't want users to be able to use ssh(1) to log on from one machine to another as root. SSH access is controlled via public key authentication,[14] which uses the various SSH_* environment variables. Allow sudo to pass these variables for `scp` alone by attaching *env_keep* statements to a rule.

```
%wheel   ALL = /usr/bin/scp env_keep += "SSH_*"
```

Also use this syntax to preserve specific variables for certain users or machines.

Retaining the User Environment

Users might need sudo to leave their precious shell environments alone. Sudo can leave the environment intact, stripping only known bad environment variables. This is yet another example of enumerating badness. Disabling this check is like removing the safety gate on an industrial meat grinder, and I strongly recommend not doing so. If you insist on jumping into the grinder and becoming sysadmin sausage, however, this is how you do it.

---

14   Some environments use only password authentication for SSH, but I'm sure all of my readers are wholesome folks and would never dream of permitting such an abomination to escape the lab.

The *env_reset* option controls resetting the environment. It tells sudo to remove all environment variables except a trusted few, and is set by default. To pass all environment variables, explicitly turn it off.

```
Defaults !env_reset
```

Now strip away the environment variables known to be risky.

Discarding Environment Variables

Many environment variables are unilaterally discarded, as they're not safe to pass through to a privileged process. The list is operating-system dependent so I won't go through it here; check the output of sudo -V for the current list on your hosts.

Most of the environment variables removed by default have one or more specific exploits associated with them. They are known to be dangerous to use with sudo. Don't reactivate these lightly. Use the *env_delete* option to adjust this list.

```
Defaults !env_reset, env_delete += "PS4 LD_LIBRARY_PATH"
```

I've retained the whole environment, except for those suspicious variables PS4 and LD_LIBRARY_PATH.

Environment Option Priority

Both *env_keep* and *env_check* override *env_delete*. An environment variable listed in both *env_keep* and *env_delete* will pass into the target environment. You shouldn't need *env_keep* or *env_check* simultaneously with *env_delete*, however; either you're allowing stuff you know to be acceptable, or you're letting everyone in except selected suspicious tidbits.

If the user has raw shell access, these protections are only temporary. The new shell could source a file containing the problem variables, or a user could just set the variables at the command prompt. But total control of the environment is part of why such users want raw privileged shell access.

Allowing User Overrides

In some cases, users might need to customize their environment in ways the policy can't anticipate. You might need a policy that grants environmental flexibility. This is especially common in test and staging environments, where some poor application administrator needs to figure out how to make the newest version of his application behave. Sudoers lets you write a security policy that says "Here are our standard environment settings, but let these specific users on these machines set their own environment variables for these commands."

The SETENV tag lets the user ask sudo to leave their environment unchanged when running the privileged command. Here, user Pete has a specific exemption allowing him to set his own privileged environment on a test host.

```
pete    dbtest1 = (pg) SETENV: ALL
```

On the machine **dbtest1**, Pete can use his own environment when running any command as the user **pg**. Pete can tweak Postgres all he wants, document his requirements, and submit a request to deploy the needed settings in production.

Sudo still defaults to resetting the environment, SETENV tag or no. Users must use the -E flag to request environment preservation.

```
# sudo -E -u pg psql
```

Without the -E flag, sudo performs its usual environment sanitizing.

In addition to the SETENV tag, there's a *setenv* option. Use it just like any other option.

```
Defaults:thea   setenv
```

Thea can use -E to override her environment on any machine. As the senior sysadmin she's already on the hook for system damage, and she claims she needs the flexibility to troubleshoot any possible problem. The ability to override her environment on demand is a legitimate exception, especially as it only works on request.

Sysadmins responsible for finicky applications that read their configuration from environment variables are painfully aware that extraneous environment variables will wreak havoc upon their carefully tuned program. Users who have permission to set their privileged environment can list specific variables to be preserved on the command line, through the --preserve-env argument. Used on its own, --preserve-env behaves exactly like -E and preserves the user's whole environment. Add an equals sign, though, and you can list specific environment variables to preserve. Here, our Postgres admin preserves three environment variables.

```
$ sudo --preserve-environment=\
  PGHOST,PGPASSFILE,PGDATABASE psql
```

Sudo discards, retains, and/or sanity-checks all other environment variables as usual, but also retains PGHOST, PGPASSFILE, and PGDATABASE.

SETENV allows users to bypass the automatic removal of dangerous environment variables. Sudo automatically strips variables like LD_LIBRARY_PATH, but a user who has SETENV can choose to retain that variable.

Give only highly trusted users the ability to retain chosen environment variables.

Target User Environment

I once sat in a meeting which boiled down to "The server runs fine, unless Dave restarts it." The administrative solution was to fire Dave or, worse, transfer him to sales. Fortunately for Dave, we had the technological solution of fixing how sudo managed Dave's environment.

In some cases you don't want to carry *any* environment settings into the privileged environment. You don't even want your shell or home directory. Rather, you need to run the command as the target user, in the target user's carefully tuned environment. Consider the database administrator from the previous section, who needs the ability to carry select parts of their environment into privileged commands in his test environment. Once they identify the application's requirements, they'll want those settings nailed down on the production server. Enable this with sudo's `-i` option.

By running a command via `sudo -i`, you simulate running the command as a new login as the target user. Sudo reads the target user's dotfiles like `.login` and `.profile`, then runs the requested command. Your original user environment is not retained in any way. Here I run the psql command as a new login.

```
$ sudo -i psql
```

In my experience, having sudo fully emulate the target user is the best way to manage applications heavily dependent on their environment. Many databases and server-side Java programs react badly to unexpected environment settings. By configuring that environment in a single account and always using that account, you eliminate one threat to application stability.

You cannot enforce use of `sudo -i` in sudo. Solaris, and Linuxes that use PAM, can use pam_env to set user-specific environments. You can use *env_file* and *restricted_env_file* to impose an environment, as we'll discuss next.

Environment Customization

A sudo policy can do more than allow and reject environment variables; it can explicitly set them. This is useful for managing environment variables like PATH and HOME, and for injecting environment variables needed to function on your network.

Adding Environment Variables

Sometimes you'll need to set environment variables for privileged commands. Use the *env_file* and *restricted_env_file* options to give the full path to a file containing the new environment variables. Suppose you want privileged commands to access the Internet via your proxy server. Create a file containing the environment variables.

```
FTP_PROXY=http://proxyhost:8080
ftp_proxy=http://proxyhost:8080
HTTP_PROXY=http://proxyhost:8080
http_proxy=http://proxyhost:8080
```

Now use the *env_file* option to add these values to the privileged environment.

```
Defaults env_file=/etc/sudo_env
```

Sudo filters the contents of *restricted_env_file* by *env_keep* and *env_check*, exactly like any other environment variables. Dangerous settings like LD_LIBRARY_PATH are discarded, while TZ and friends get sanity-checked.

As a final step in setting up the privileged command environment, sudo adds the contents of *env_file*. Unlike *restricted_env_file*, the contents of this file are completely trusted. You can set LD_LIBRARY_PATH or TZ in *env_file*.

If these environment variables already exist in the user's environment before running sudo, sudo will not replace them.

Managing PATH

An intruder who can get a sabotaged binary on a system often tries to sabotage a user's PATH, so that the user runs the bogus command rather that the proper one. If a helpdesk flunky needs to reset a user's password, but runs `/tmp/.1234/hacker/passwd` rather than `/usr/bin/passwd`, bad things happen. This attack happens most often when the ALL command alias is in use. Use the *secure_path* and *ignore_dot* options to define your trusted path for sudo commands.

```
Defaults secure_path="/bin /usr/bin /sbin /usr/sbin"
```

Sudo tries to run the desired command using the secure path. If the command isn't in the path, it fails. The user can still run the command by typing the full path, but hopefully your helpdesk would notice something wrong if they had to run `/tmp/.1234/hacker/passwd thea`.

The *secure_path* option affects commands run via sudo, but not shell instances. If you start a full interactive shell via `sudo su -` or `sudo -i`, the shell reads the target user's startup shell files and initializes the target user's standard PATH.

While *secure_path* assures that commands run under sudo are in the system's standard program directories, it does nothing to ensure that the user is running the proper sudo command. Users still must care for their PATH if they don't want to run `/tmp/.1234/hacker/sudo`.

The *ignore_dot* option strips any . entries from PATH when running sudo. Some users like to have the current directory included in their PATH, but if someone could get a bogus copy of `passwd` into the helpdesk account's home directory there would be trouble. The *ignore_dot* option is on by default. If you want to allow the dot in PATH when running sudo commands, disable it (*!ignore_dot*).

Managing HOME

Privileged commands might dump sensitive files in the user's home directory, or expect to find critical files in that directory. Sudo normally sets HOME to the target user's home directory. Allowing users to retain their HOME or disabling environment resets might cause core files containing decrypted passwords to appear in the user's home directory. This would be bad. When you leave the user's environment otherwise unchanged, enforce setting HOME to that of the target user with the *always_set_home* option.

```
Defaults         !env_reset,always_set_home
```

Here the user's environment is left unchanged, except for setting HOME to that of the target user.

Users can use the -H flag to request that sudo set HOME to the target user's home directory.

```
$ sudo -u pg -H psql
```

Again, this is the default; it's needed only when sudo's environment reset is disabled.

Managing Pagers

A *pager* is the program that displays long output one screen at a time. The standard Unix pager these days is less(1), and all sorts of software uses it to manage output. Programmers cannot resist adding new features to pagers, though, which is why less has features like "examine another file," "feed this output to another command," and "become a fully functional Turing machine capable of running DOOM." Fortunately, the designers of less knew these features could be trouble and included a toggle to turn them off. It's controlled via environment variables. As if this wasn't enough, lots of other pagers support these same features.

Running less in "secure mode" requires setting the environment variable LESSSECURE, and then imposing the use of less as a pager through the environment variables PAGER and MANPAGER. Sudo will not set these environment variables if they exist in the user's environment, so tell sudoers to never allow them to remain in the user environment.

```
Defaults env_delete+= "PAGER MANPAGER LESSSECURE"
```

Once you've stripped out possibly bogus settings, add in trusted values. Create an environment file that contains your settings. Here's my */etc/sudo_pager_env*.

```
LESSSECURE=1
PAGER=less
MANPAGER=less
```

Now add it to your sudoers policy.

```
Defaults env_file += "/etc/sudo_pager_env"
```

I use += to allow me to add other environment files to certain hosts, users, or commands.

With these settings, the system's pager program is no longer a menace. Unless the user has privileged access to env(1) and can have it run other programs and strip out inconvenient environment variables—or, worse, run `env /bin/sh`.

Running Shells with Sudo

Some folks use sudo with su(1), allowing them to get a privileged shell with their own password instead of the root password.

```
$ sudo su
```

I strongly discourage this. Routinely running a privileged shell is poor practice, for reasons discussed in innumerable articles and ignored by innumerable younger sysadmins.[15] If you haven't learned that lesson yet, read on.

Sudo logs which commands people run, but without additional configuration sudo doesn't log what happens inside a shell session. (We'll cover sudo logging in Chapter 12). But since some of you insist on doing exactly this, let's discuss it.

The `su` command means "switch user." Running `su -` or `su -l` initializes a new shell, giving you the target user's environment. Running plain `su` switches the user you're running as but retains most of your environment.

If you want to completely replace su with sudo, you could enable the *shells_noargs* option. With this set, running sudo with no arguments gives you a root command prompt.

```
Defaults:thea shell_noargs
```

When senior sysadmin Thea runs sudo without any command-line arguments, she's root.

```
$ sudo
Password:
#
```

If your account doesn't have *shell_noargs* access, but you can run shells, simulate a login as the target user by using sudo's `-s` flag. It's like running `su -`.

```
$ sudo -s
Password:
#
```

---

[15] I see no need to argue this point, however. Sooner or later, reality will persuade you.

If the user does not have permission to run the root account's shell, sudo denies access even if *shell_noargs* is present.

Which should you use? Ideally, none. If you must let users become another user via sudo, configure complete session logging as per Chapter 12.

Terminals and Graphic Interfaces

You can use sudo to manage commands on graphical desktops, when there's no command prompt. You can run sudo without a terminal, or demand that a command only run in a terminal. You can even use sudo for backgrounded commands. All of these require understanding what's really happening, though, and some uses demand additional configuration.

No Terminal

Your fancy graphic desktop interface probably lets you right-click and pick a program to run, or double-click an icon to run a command. Some of those commands probably need sudo. How can you enter your password when you don't have a terminal window to enter it in? That's where the askpass function comes in.

Sudo can run an external program to provide a password prompt. All Unix systems support a variety of these programs, and your window manager might even have an integrated one. We'll use the standard OpenSSH program for requesting a password, openssh-askpass(1). Use `sudo.conf` to tell sudo the path to the askpass program.

```
Path askpass /usr/local/bin/ssh-askpass
```

When sudo needs a password and doesn't have a terminal, it fires up the askpass program to request one. If the askpass program can't run either, sudo fails.

If you want to trigger the askpass program in a terminal window, use the -A flag to sudo.

```
$ sudo -A cat /var/log/auth.log
```

Either the askpass program will pop up, or you'll get an error message that (hopefully) explains why the askpass program can't pop up.

If you want to unilaterally disable all of sudo's requests for input, including password, use sudo with the -n flag. If sudo needs a password, it dies.

Requiring a Terminal

Daemons like cron and databases and even web servers might run other programs. These programs run as child processes, without a login shell. This means they don't have a terminal. And sometimes you'll want sudo to only run certain commands when there's a terminal present. Instruct sudo to require, or disallow, running a command in a terminal through the *requiretty* option.

Setting *requiretty* tells sudo to only allow the command if it's run in a terminal. Enabling this in sudoers means that the program cannot run without a terminal.

```
Defaults!/usr/bin/passwd requiretty
```

Someone might trick the host's web server to change a password, but without a terminal it won't work.

While *requiretty* is off by default on a majority of Unixes, a few Unixes have defaulted to only allowing sudo to run when there's a terminal. You can disable *requiretty* to allow these Unixes to behave like every other Unix.

```
Defaults !requiretty
```

Many programs, such as OpenSSH, have features to allocate a terminal even if it's not needed.

Backgrounding Commands

Running commands in the background is one of Unix's most powerful features. Sudo supports running commands in the background with the –b flag. Yes, you could use CTRL-Z and bg(1) to suspend and background a running process, or start a process with nohup(1), but if you know in advance you want to do that, use –b.

```
$ sudo -b tail -f /var/log/auth.log
```

Sudo prompts for your password in the foreground, then backgrounds the privileged command.

The catch with backgrounding commands via sudo is that you can't use standard job control to re-foreground them. You need to kill the privileged process instead.

Timeouts

You can tell sudo to enforce a timeout on privileged commands. If a program runs longer than the timeout, sudo kills it. Set this up with the *command_timeout* option.

```
Defaults          command_timeout=10
```

If a command runs longer than 10 seconds, sudo kills it.

A numerical timeout without any unit is in seconds. Timeouts can also be specified in days (d), hours (h), minutes (m), seconds (s), or any combination of these. You can omit any of these from a timeout, but they must be listed from largest unit to smallest. A timeout of 7d1s is seven days and one second, but 1s7d is not valid. Sudo timeouts have no syntax for weeks or months, so 7m1w is also invalid. Setting a timeout to zero disables the timeout.

Attach a timeout to a command using TIMEOUT. This looks a lot like a tag, but there's no colon.

```
thea              ALL = TIMEOUT=4h ALL
```

We'll use Defaults until we start working with LDAP, to avoid cluttering our privileges.

Timeouts as Soft Policy Enforcement

Use timeouts to discourage people from logging in as root while not explicitly blocking them from doing so. Consider this policy.

```
Defaults            command_timeout=10
Cmnd_Alias    SHELL=/bin/sh, /bin/csh, /bin/tcsh,\
    /usr/bin/su,/bin/sudo
Defaults!SHELL    command_timeout=2m
Defaults!/usr/local/bin/visudo command_timeout=5m
Defaults@thea     command_timeout=0
```

The default command timeout is ten seconds.

The SHELL alias contains programs that let a user have a root shell. These programs may run for up to two minutes before sudo terminates them. Two minutes is enough to carry out brief tasks where you truly need root, but short enough that it's not worth logging in as root for routine use. We're not enumerating badness here: explicitly listed programs get a *longer* timeout than other programs.

We set a longer timeout for programs that need it, such as visudo.

Lastly, senior sysadmin Thea can have any program, including a privileged shell, open as long as necessary. She doesn't expect to need one, but if things go terribly wrong she'll need it.

You'll discover additional programs that need to run longer, and will probably also need special rules. When I'm debugging issues I'll often run `tail -f` on log files. Such commands should have a timeout of a few hours, but should also be tagged NOEXEC.

User Timeouts

A user might want to set a timeout on their own commands. This could be because they're responsible administrators, or it could be because it helps restrain badly programmed software. Allow a user to set a timeout with the *user_command_timeout* option.

```
Defaults    user_command_timeout
```

The user can now set a timeout with sudo's -T flag.

If *command_timeout* is set, the user timeout cannot exceed it. A user can request a timeout longer than that set by *command_timeout*, but that request will not be honored. If *command_timeout* is set to one minute but the user requests a one hour timeout, the command will be terminated in one minute.

You can now fold, spindle, and mutilate sudo's privileged environment. Now let's see how sudo can protect your users from a damaged system.

"Good morning, I am a hacker. Er, please don't panic, just hand over /usr/bin/passwd."

Chapter 9: Intrusion Detection

One of the problems mentioned in the previous chapter is that of an intruder tampering with PATH. Sanitizing PATH helps, but what if our bad actor replaces the actual `/usr/bin/passwd` with his own treacherous version? Sudo can verify the *cryptographic digest* (or *checksum*, or *hash*) of a command before running it, preventing these kinds of attacks.

Why is this useful? A cryptographic digest is a mathematical transformation that creates a long fixed-length string for any chunk of data. Even minor changes in the file dramatically change the file's digest. If sudo knows that the correct digest for the legitimate passwd program is X, but the passwd program has a digest of Y, sudo will refuse to run.

An intruder is not the only one who might alter the file containing a command. If you have write access to the directory containing the command, you might accidentally alter it yourself. A user frustrated by system restrictions might try to evade those restrictions. "I know how to fix this, I just need root!"[16]

Digest verification can prevent you from running a copy of `dd` that someone accidentally copied over the `mv` command. Would running that hurt anything? Probably not, unless you need to move some very

---

16   This is also known as "Management Won't Let Me Do My Job Syndrome," which is not improved by developing "I Gave Them An Excuse To Fire Me Disorder."

oddly named files. But such errors can be catastrophic, and they're the first sign that an operating system instance is badly damaged. Digest verification offers early warning of possible system damage.

System upgrades change digests. If you deploy digest verification, updating digests must be part of your upgrade process. You'll need a way to update sudoers without sudo, or write a specific sudo rule that lets your automation system install new digests.

Using digests to verify command integrity has three steps: choosing an algorithm, generating the digests, and writing a sudoers rule that validates the digest.

Digest Algorithm

Sudo supports several variants of SHA digests: SHA-224, SHA-256, SHA-384, and SHA-512. Higher numbers mean that the digest is more difficult to reverse-engineer, but creating and validating the digest takes more computing power. Most systems have more processor power than they know what to do with, however, so I use SHA-512. All SHA-512 digests are 128 characters.

If you have strong opinions on the merits of different SHA digests, feel free to choose what complies with your prejudices. Realistically, all of these algorithms provide sufficient protection against all practical attacks.[17]

Generating Digests

Unix-like systems offer several ways to compute digests, and they're all slightly different. Most offer either sha512(1) or sha512sum(1) for computing the SHA512 digest of a file. Here I use Linux's `sha512sum` to get the digest of `/usr/bin/passwd`.

17　If an Evil Secret Agent wants to compromise your computer, she won't bother replacing binaries with treacherous versions carefully engineered to have the same digest. Access to the Super Fast Digest Cracking Hardware[tm] requires too much paperwork. She'll use your kneecaps. And a hammer.

```
$ sha512sum /usr/bin/passwd
fa73ee2b8e7ddbaa343b5adb7432bb5a8d453a3c8a5b50f9df510c6
94c7f9ce7688c0f1e493fe116efb1958258ce3515185d20f2f2684f
4c0b05200f3b62091c  /usr/bin/passwd
```

The horrid string beginning with *fa73* and ending with *091c* is the digest. I'll trim the digests in the rest of my examples so your eyes don't bleed.

You can also use openssl(1) to generate digests. It's available almost everywhere, but the command line is slightly uglier.

```
$ openssl dgst -sha512 /sbin/shutdown
```

Use whatever's most convenient in your environment.

Digests in Sudoers

A cryptographic digest is a tag added to a command. Before the command name, give the digest type, a colon, and the digest. Unless you have multiple commands with identical digests, you need one rule per command.

```
%helpdesk ALL = sha512:fa73…091c /usr/bin/passwd
```

When someone in the helpdesk group asks to run passwd(1), sudo computes the SHA-512 digest for */usr/bin/passwd*. If the generated digest matches the digest in the sudoers rule, sudo runs the command. Otherwise, the user gets the generic "not allowed" message. If `sudo -l` shows that you have permission to run the command, but every attempt to do so gives you a "not allowed" message, the digest of the command file doesn't match the command's sudoers entry.

If multiple binaries have the same digest, you probably goofed. Double-check the command you used to produce the digest. If multiple program files truly have the same digest they might be the same binary linked to by multiple names, such as Sendmail and its posse. List commands with identical digests together like so.

```
Cmnd_Alias SENDMAIL = sha512:06a2...c62a \
    /usr/sbin/sendmail, /usr/bin/mailq, \
    /usr/sbin/hoststat, /usr/bin/newaliases
```

No matter what name the program is called by, they all go to the same binary and thus have the same checksum.

Multiple Operating Systems

If you're centralizing your sudoers policy and want to deploy digest verification, you'll need a policy that permits multiple digests for a single command. The digest for Debian's `sendmail` binary differs from `sendmail` on FreeBSD. Even on the same operating system, digests vary between patchlevels.

How can you cope with this? Use one command alias per operating system.

```
Cmnd_Alias FB_13_0_SENDMAIL = sha512:81bc...f9a1 \
    /usr/sbin/sendmail, /usr/bin/mailq, \
    /usr/sbin/hoststat, /usr/bin/newaliases
Cmnd_Alias DEBIAN_9_9_SENDMAIL = sha512:c0da...14fc \
    /usr/sbin/sendmail, /usr/bin/mailq, \
    /usr/bin/newaliases
Cmnd_Alias SENDMAIL = \
    FB_13_0_SENDMAIL, DEBIAN_9_9_SENDMAIL
```

This takes a hideous-looking policy statement and multiplies its awfulness by the number of operating systems and patchlevels you're running, and multiplies that by the number of commands on the system. It is an offense to the eye and a burden upon the spirit. That means it's a perfect job for Perl.

Automating Checksum-Aware Sudoers

Performing checksum validation upon your sudoers policy is overkill for enterprises with a single host. I only do this when I have a small test lab where I can replicate my production environments and produce the sudoers policy, and automation where I can push out new sudoers files along with updates. This requires tricky management of the sudoers policy, so that you don't wind up trying to use a policy for OS version X when you're running X+1. In my world, that meant installing a temporary sudo policy that gave the automation user full sudo access, installing the operating system updates, installing the new digest files and policies, and removing the automation's full access. Consider the right solution for your environment before proceeding; you might have something more clever.[18]

If this doesn't scare you off, my code might. But follow along anyway.

The code I present here makes perfect sense for my systems. Always consider your environment and make appropriate changes before using sample code.

Automatic creation of a checksum-aware sudoers has three parts: building a command alias (including the checksum) for every program on the system, building a master command alias that includes all of those commands, and building user rules using those aliases. Use a separate script for each.

Creating Command Aliases with Checksums

I wrote the script `sudodigest.pl` to generate digests. Rather than trying to copy it from this book, grab a copy from my book github (https://www.github.com/mwlucas/) or, better still, write your own, improved script.

My sudoers are used across operating systems, such as different Linux distributions or different BSD variants. (Yes, some folks work in operating system monocultures, and I feel sorry for them.) These files will be generated in a staging area and distributed to the servers through a central automation system. We must be able to clearly differentiate aliases for Debian from OpenBSD, not to mention the various patch levels of CentOS 9.9 even though CentOS doesn't *have* patch lev-

---

18   Sysadmin Rule #5: "Cleverness" is directly proportional to "fragility."

els. In my environment, it's sensible to use uname -s and uname -r to build these alias names. Then the alias name needs the full path to the command, to differentiate identically named commands in different directories. We compute the digest of each command, add it to the policy statement, and add the path to the command.

This sounds pretty simple, but there's lots of catches. Sudo aliases can only contain capital letters, numbers, and underscores. Some command names have periods in them, or dashes, or plus signs. The right bracket ([) is a perfectly legitimate and, indeed, necessary command. We can't just uppercase all the names—remember mail and Mail, or cc and CC? Any script must do a bunch of substitution and sanitization to create unique and valid alias names.

If you do use this script, adjust the contents of *@directories* to include only the directories you want to checksum.

```
#!/usr/bin/env perl
#Generate sudo checksums and aliases for all programs in
a directory.

#Put list of directories here
@directories = ("/bin","/sbin","/usr/bin","/usr/sbin",\
    "/usr/local/bin", "/usr/local/sbin");
#figure out OS & patchlevel to put in front of our
#commands, to make aliases unique, and add that to top
#of output for use by Future Me

chomp($os= `uname -s`); #what OS are we running
chomp($patchlevel=`uname -r`); #current release

print "#Generated for $os $patchlevel\n#\n\n";

foreach $directory (@directories) {

    #we need a label for the directory, separate from
    #the directory
    $pathlabel=$directory;
    $pathlabel=~s#/##g;
    #assemble prefix for command name
    $prefix="$os-$patchlevel-$pathlabel-";
```

```perl
#aliases can only contain [A-Z0-9_], sanitize to that
$prefix = uc $prefix;
$prefix =~ s/[^A-Z0-9_]/_/g;

#We can now process individual directory entries and
#produce sudoers digest lines
opendir (DIRECTORY, $directory);
while ( $file = readdir (DIRECTORY)) {
   if($file eq "." || $file eq ".."){ next;}

   my $literalpath="$directory/$file";

   #/usr/bin/mail and /usr/bin/Mail both exist,
   #because life hates me. Can't share alias names,
   #so put a _ in front of every capital letter in the
   #filename.
   $file =~ s#([A-Z])#_\1#g;

   #Build & sanitize command alias
   my $file = uc $file;
   my $CmndAlias="${prefix}$file";
   $CmndAlias=~s#[.]#DOT#g;
   $CmndAlias=~s#[+]#PLUS#g;
   $CmndAlias=~s#[-]#DASH#g;
   $CmndAlias=~s#[[]#LBRACKET#g;

   print "Cmnd_Alias $CmndAlias = sha512:";

   if ($os=~/BSD/) {
  #we use sha512(1)
  chomp ($digest=`/sbin/sha512 -q $literalpath`);
  print "$digest ";
  print $literalpath;
  print "\n";

   }
 if ($os=~/Linux/) {
   #we use sha512sum(1)
   $digest=`/usr/bin/sha512sum $literalpath`;
   print $digest;

   }
  }
}
#Now use ids-sudoers.pl to build sample policies
```

This produces a whole bunch of sudo aliases like the one below.

```
Cmnd_Alias FREEBSD_12_0_RELEASE_P6_BIN_SH = sha512:a19a...0057 /bin/sh
```

By referring to the command alias FREEBSD_12_0_RELEASE_P6_BIN_SH, you're referencing /bin/sh with a specific checksum, as deployed on FreeBSD 12.0-p6. Linux releases get similar labels based on the kernel version.

Referring to these labels in your policy isn't much better, so we need to generate our policy rules programmatically as well.

Creating a Master Alias

Probably the most commonly deployed sudo rule is "If the user is in the correct group, give them unrestricted sudo access." This script, digest-everything.pl, creates an alias that contains every sudo command that we've created a checksum for and gives the administrative groups access to that alias. It takes one argument, a sudoers alias file created by sudodigest.pl. I simplify the code[19] by including the command /nonexistent at the end of the alias. Many servers and accounts for daemons use /nonexistent as a location that's known to not exist.

```perl
#!/usr/bin/env perl
#Takes a digested list of command aliases and builds a
#couple of sample sudoers policies from them. Takes one
#argument, a file containing digested aliases.

die unless (open (DIGESTS, $ARGV[0]));

print "Cmnd_Alias EVERYTHING = ";

while (<DIGESTS>) {
   chomp;
   next unless /^Cmnd_Alias/;
   my ($discard, $CmndAlias, $equal, $hash, $command) =
   split;
   print "$CmndAlias, ";
}
```

---

19   aka "cheat"

```
#An alias cannot end with a comma, so list a non-
#runnable non-existent thing at the end
print "/nonexistent\n\n";

#support both wheel and sudo groups for cross-platform
print "%wheel ALL= EVERYTHING\n";
print "%sudo ALL= EVERYTHING\n";
```

Give this script one argument, the sudo policy file containing the digests generated by `sudodigest.pl`. The resulting policy looks like this.

```
Cmnd_Alias EVERYTHING = \
   FREEBSD_12_0_RELEASE_P6_BIN_CHIO, \
   FREEBSD_12_0_RELEASE_P6_BIN_KILL, \
   ...
   FREEBSD_12_0_RELEASE_P6_USRLOCALSBIN_VISUDO, \
   /nonexistent

%wheel ALL= EVERYTHING
%sudo ALL= EVERYTHING
```

We have the alias EVERYTHING, which goes on for several pages. The last two lines give users in the **wheel** and **sudo** groups unlimited access to all the programs. These users can't run any program on the system, only those in digested directories.

They could run shells, though. It would be nice to use an exclusion rule to eliminate the shells, but Chapter 3 really hammered on how excluding shells from a policy doesn't work.

Here's the trick, though. While enumerating badness always fails, the EVERYTHING alias is an explicit list of programs that presumably contains zero known badness. Every program in EVERYTHING is an approved, installed program. A user could copy /bin/sh to /tmp/sh, but there's no sudo rule allowing /tmp/sh to be run as root. You could have a rule like this.

```
%wheel ALL = NOEXEC:EVERYTHING, \
   !/bin/sh, !/bin/bash, !/usr/bin/su
```

Admin users get slightly less goodness, but still an awful lot of privilege—provided you can keep track of which shells are installed on your system.

Custom Aliases

Complete automation of alias creation isn't realistic. Senior sysadmin Thea just wants to assign someone to run the backups. And she's not going to bother with horrible long alias names either. We need automation to create more human-friendly aliases that group commands by job role. Consider the basic command alias from Chapter 3, which put three commands in one handy unit.

```
Cmnd_Alias    BACKUP=/sbin/dump,/sbin/restore,/usr/bin/mt
mike          ALL=BACKUP
```

Managing the second line, assigning users the rights to the BACKUP commands, is trivial. She could assign someone else that tedious job any time. But to perform digest verification, either the BACKUP alias needs to be defined using the aliases that have digests assigned to them or we need to give those digests in the first line.

The solution here is to separate creation of the command alias BACKUP and the rule assigning users and groups that role. Assign duties in a hand-maintained file, but automatically generate the BACKUP alias.

This script, `backup-alias.pl`, generates the BACKUP alias. It looks an awful lot like `digest-everything.pl`.

```perl
#!/usr/bin/env perl

#Takes a digested list of command aliases and builds an #alias named
BACKUP containing select commands

die unless (open (DIGESTS, $ARGV[0]));
print "Cmnd_Alias BACKUP = ";
while (<DIGESTS>) {
    chomp;
    next unless /^Cmnd_Alias/;
    my ($discard, $CmndAlias, $equal, $hash, $command) = split;
    next unless \
        ( $command=~m'^/sbin/dump$|^/sbin/restore$|^/usr/bin/mt$' );
    print "$CmndAlias, ";
}
#An alias cannot end with a comma, so list a
#non-runnable non-existent thing at the end
print "/nonexistent\n\n";
```

Run this, giving an argument of the digests command file produced by `sudodigest.pl`, and you'll produce something like this.

```
Cmnd_Alias BACKUP = FREEBSD_12_0_RELEASE_P6_SBIN_DUMP,\
  FREEBSD_12_0_RELEASE_P6_SBIN_RESTORE, \
  FREEBSD_12_0_RELEASE_P6_USRBIN_MT, /nonexistent
```

You can easily modify or expand the script to produce human-friendly aliases for any set of digests aliases. When you deploy your policy with NOEXEC, create a script that creates an exception alias for programs like newaliases and visudo that must EXEC. The more you automate your policy, the easier it will be to update.

Putting It All Together

All these scripts are nice, but they still need to be run. The best way to run a mass of scripts… is to script them. I use a master script to manage all these smaller scripts.

```
#!/bin/sh

cd /etc/sudoers.d.tmp/
sudodigest.pl > 00-digests
digest-everything.pl 00-digests > 10-everything
backup-alias.pl 00-digests > 10-backup
helpdesk-alias.pl 00-digests > 10-helpdesk
exec-alias.pl 00-digests > 10-exec
...
```

The digests file begins with 00, so sudo reads it first. All our general aliases are maintained in files starting with 10. This leaves every number greater than 10 for human-readable rules, all protected with digest verification.

As mentioned when starting this chapter, the tricky part of managing digest verification involves getting all these rules onto all your local machines. It's much better to design one policy and then distribute it to the rest of the network, as discussed in the next chapter.

> *"You browse at your peril, for I have two servers here. I know one of them isn't running any more, but the other one is, so that's one of you DDOS'd for sure… or just about for sure anyway. It certainly wouldn't be worth your while risking it because I'm a very good sysadmin."*

Chapter 10: Policy Distribution

On a single machine, any non-trivial sudo configuration is a lot of trouble. If you run hundreds or thousands of servers, however, sudo makes user privileges way more manageable. Not easy or simple, but manageable. The best way to have a consistent policy across your network is to write a single sudoers policy and replicate it to all machines on the network. Most large sites use configuration management tools to distribute files across their server farms. If you're not there yet, consider tools like rsync. This is a long-running problem; in 1986, BSD included rdist(1) for exactly this purpose.

Writing a single central policy used across all your machines means paying careful attention to safe and secure policies.

Global Policy Hints

We've touched on how to escape sudo's restrictions in many places, but let's consider them all together as a "greatest hits" of how to write, and *not* write, sudoer policies.

Create aliases for users, commands, hosts, and RunAs settings. Write your rules using those aliases. Changes to aliases propagate coherently through the policy and maintain consistency.

The most frequent problem with a sudo policy is the command list. Many sysadmins have no problems restricting access to specific users and hosts, but crumble and fail when it comes to the command list.

The command alias ALL grants users who can copy or create files unlimited privileged access. Users can trivially bypass command lists like `ALL`, `!/bin/sh`, and NOEXEC doesn't work on static binaries. ALL means absolutely everything. If you're thinking of restricting ALL, don't bother using it. Enumerating badness always fails. Instead, create lists of commands that users can run—and don't include any commands that users can write to in that list! If you want to allow all but a few commands, use a script like that in Chapter 3 to generate an alias containing all commands and then trim it.

Set *noexec* as a default (Chapter 5). Specifically enumerate commands that must have access to run other commands. This helps eliminate problems like `env bash`.

Force use of less(1) as a pager, and lock it down as per Chapter 8.

Hesitate to give root-level privileges to shell scripts via sudo. While sudo sanitizes the privileged shell environment, a shell script can put that scary stuff right in. In too many cases, running a script as root via sudo is equivalent to giving the user root. Use digests (Chapter 9) to enforce script integrity, as well as that of any scripts called by those scripts. Users and intruders can subvert any number of shell scripts with environment variables. Don't think that your users are different and won't mess around with your carefully written shell scripts. They aren't and they will.

On some hosts, a tight sudo configuration is unrealistic. General-purpose desktop machines run many programs that run other programs. Test and development hosts exist specifically to try new things. A user who has physical access to the machine can get root access without much difficulty. Your best practice is to assume that such machines are untrustworthy and secure your servers against both internal and external attackers.

Often, sysadmins don't really know what commands they need to do their job. As with so many other careers, they're so familiar with their tools that using them is almost unconscious. If you have a group of users you want to migrate from using the root password, start by giving them unrestricted sudo privileges for a defined period and retaining the logs. This allows you to organically develop a list of commands that your sysadmins use. That list is a big step towards a real policy, or at least a discussion of why routinely running `rm -rf` as root is poor practice.

If you're not willing to do the work of creating a real sudoers policy, then don't waste your time slapping together a half-cocked sudoers policy that sort of, more or less, kind of does what you want, basically. Instead, set up full session logging (Chapter 12), give users ALL, and deal with the fallout. After enough unnecessary downtime, system damage, and lost nights and weekends, your organization will give you the support needed to develop a real sudoers policy.

Finally, use comments. Note when the policy was written, when it was installed, and who installed it. List change control revisions. List anything that will help people figure out why the policy doesn't work as they expect. Comments are free, use them liberally.

Now that you have the determination and support to create that policy, here are hints on how to write it.

Hostnames and Sudoers

When managing sudoers individually on each machine, the hostname part of the policy tends to disappear from the sysadmin's view. It's still in the file, but your conscious mind no longer perceives it. It becomes "that '*ALL =*' thing" that must appear in the middle of each rule. Even this book hasn't given it much attention so far. When you want to use a single policy across your network, the hostname field gets a whole bunch more important.

Sudo gets the name of the local machine by running `hostname`. The hostname in your sudoers policy must exactly match whatever hostname the local machine thinks it is. Some Unixes give their hostname as a single word, such as **www8** or **lucaslaptop**. Others offer fully qualified domain names, like **mail.mwl.io**. Which Unixes use which? That changes over time, as distributors and developers change their minds how their Unix should function. Before you start writing your centralized policy, investigate hostnames as they actually appear on your real servers. Are they consistent? Can you change them to be consistent? Rationalizing all your hostnames and their naming schemes will save you long term pain.

Or, use DNS or IP addresses.

DNS and Sudoers

The Domain Name System (DNS) maps hostnames to IP addresses and back. A server can think its name is **www8**, but the DNS tells the outside world its name is **www8.mwl.io**. DNS is centrally managed, mostly. Having sudo refer to DNS for machine names removes any local host name inconsistencies. It also adds a dependency on DNS for managing servers. If your DNS servers fail, sudo will not work. If sudo won't run because DNS is down, and you can't restart DNS because you can't sudo, congratulations! You failed to think through all possible failure modes. Expect your local Thea to come for your carcass shortly.

Hosts might be configured to resolve IP addresses and hostnames from a variety of information sources, such as LDAP or the hosts file, `/etc/hosts`. Some networks are probably still using YP or other Bronze Age technologies. If the server prefers one of these information sources, make sure they're consistent as well. Be sure to check `/etc/nsswitch.conf` and `/etc/host.conf` to see where your server gets its name information from.

Whatever information source you're using, it must be pristine. Mismatches between forward and reverse nameservice can cause sudo to apply policy incorrectly. Name services might offer multiple hostnames for a single host, but sudo uses only the primary host name. It ignores all aliases or additional records, but will accept multiple addresses for one hostname. If you're using the hosts file, only the first host name in an entry gets used. If you're using DNS, sudo uses only the hostnames shown in forward DNS. It ignores any CNAME records (aliases), because DNS has no way to provide a complete list of aliases.

To enable DNS in sudo, use the sudoers option *fqdn*.

```
Defaults    fqdn
```

Whenever you run sudo, it checks the local host name. If a policy statement applies to that hostname, it matches. If the name doesn't match, sudo fires up DNS and compares each rule to the server's fully qualified host name (without the ending period DNS purists might expect). You must list fully qualified domain names in policy statements. Your sudoers lines will be a little longer. Also, sudo will run slightly slower as it queries the network for name information. The hostname `localhost` gets ignored, unless that's the host's canonical name as returned by running `hostname`.

```
%helpdesk     www.mwl.io   = HELPDESK
```

Users in the `helpdesk` group can run commands in the HELPDESK alias, but only on the machine `www.mwl.io`.

While sudoers policy statements are processed in order, with the last matching rule having priority, the *fqdn* option is always processed first. Putting *fqdn* anywhere in your policy means that the whole policy relies on nameservice.

The obvious way to break hostname-based protections is for the sysadmin to change the local host's name. If your sudoers policy permits an otherwise unprivileged user to change the hostname, he can change the policy applied to the machine. Someone with that degree of access probably has any number of ways to gain root access without going anywhere near sudo, however. If this is a risk for you, use IP addresses rather than hostnames.

IP Addresses

You can identify hosts by IP address in sudoers. I find this more reliable than relying on DNS. Sudo queries every network interface. If the address is attached to any interface, the policy statement applies. Sudo ignores the loopback interface, the localhost addresses 127.0.0.1 and ::1, and any addresses attached to loopback interfaces.

```
mike    192.0.2.15 = ALLCOMMANDS
```

If your network is large enough that you need to write rules by IP addresses, you almost certainly need host aliases.

```
Host_Alias    BACKUP \
    198.51.100.10, 198.51.100.11, 198.51.100.12
```

Many large organizations have separate network subnets for different server roles. Web servers might be on one subnet, while database servers might be behind a firewall on another subnet. List IP networks in sudoers policies to capture entire swaths of machines at once.

```
Host_Alias DB    203.0.113.0/24
Host_Alias WWW   192.0.2.0/24, 2001:db8:bad:face:1::/64
```

Assign well-written access rules to these host aliases, and the only way a problem user like myself is going to get extra access via sudo is by moving the host to another subnet.

If a host has multiple IP addresses, and the policy's rules for each address conflict, the last matching rule applies.

One Network, One Sudoers

If you run hundreds of machines, you already have a way to distribute files to all of them. Tools such as Ansible and Puppet make this almost easy. Using include directories lets you update policies piecemeal, or include special files for only certain roles or operating systems.

If you're centrally managing sudo, I strongly recommend having each local machine validate the new sudoers file before installing it as `/etc/sudoers`. If you write a sudoers on a machine running sudo 1.8.41 and install it on a server running sudo 1.8.27, you might include options, tags, or features that the older sudo cannot recognize. If sudo cannot parse `/etc/sudoers`, it won't run. Having the target machine run `visudo -cf sudoers.tmp` on the new file before copying it into place will save you heaps of trouble. Search out Jan-Piet Mens' blog post "Don't try this at the office: /etc/sudoers" and the linked posts for a very good description of exactly how much pain a bad sudoers policy causes on a large network.[20]

While the sudoers syntax has remained fairly stable for years now, the most likely change is new options. The sudoers option *ignore_unknown_defaults* tells sudo to skip options it doesn't recognize. Suppose one day sudo adds the ability to call an external database file for insults using the *custominsult* option. You want to deploy this on your hosts, but some hosts don't have a new enough sudo.

---

20   It's hilarious, because it happened to someone else.

```
Defaults ignore_unknown_defaults
Defaults insults
Defaults custominsult=/etc/insult.db
```

The visudo on older hosts cannot validate this file—it knows nothing about this "custominsult" option. Sudo can't parse the option either, but thanks to *ignore_unknown_defaults* it shrugs and says "Yeah, whatever, here's your insult."

Be aware that *ignore_unknown_defaults* will not save you from other parsing errors, such as stray comments or misspelled commands.

Transforming and Filtering Sudoers

The sudo policy is a critical security document. Security information should not be distributed any further than needed. If you push a single all-inclusive sudoers out to all of your hosts, an intruder who cracks one system could review */etc/sudoers* and learn how your organization manages its servers. Many security officers object, with good reason.

Sudo includes a tool for transforming the sudoers file, cvtsudoers(1). It can filter a sudoers file based on hostname, users, or groups. It can also transform a sudoers policy into JSON or LDAP-friendly LDIF (see Chapter 11). We'll experiment with transforming sudoers in a few different ways.

A Sample Policy

Most sysadmins can transform a two-line policy into a different but familiar format without involving their brain. Transformations become interesting when you have a complex policy, however. Consider this simple sudoers, built out of a bunch of pieces previously discussed and stored in the file */etc/global-sudoers*.

```
Defaults noexec, env_keep += "SSH_*"
Defaults command_timeout=10
Defaults!SHELL command_timeout=2m
Defaults!/usr/bin/visudo command_timeout=5m
Defaults@thea  !noexec,command_timeout=4h

#hosts
Host_Alias WWW = www1, www2, www3
Host_Alias DB = db1, db2, db3

#users
User_Alias         TAPEMONKEYS=mike, pete, hank
User_Alias         DBADMIN=fred, kate
User_Alias         WWWADMIN=adel, matt, nils

#commands
Cmnd_Alias         MAYEXEC = /usr/bin/newaliases, \
    /usr/local/sbin/visudo
Cmnd_Alias         BACKUP=/sbin/dump, /sbin/restore, \
    /usr/bin/mt
Cmnd_Alias         SHELL=/bin/sh,/bin/csh,/bin/tcsh,\
    /bin/bash,/usr/bin/su,/usr/local/bin/sudo

#runas
Runas_Alias        DBUSER=pg,mysql

#rules

TAPEMONKEYS        ALL=BACKUP
DBADMIN   DB = (DBUSER) ALL
WWWADMIN WWW = ALL

%wheel             ALL = (ALL) ALL
%wheel             ALL = EXEC:MAYEXEC,SHELL
```

This policy sets defaults sensible for our environment, such as retaining SSH environment variables and *noexec*. Command timeouts keep our users from having privileged commands run indefinitely. We define teams who support backups, database servers, and web servers. Database administrators can run any command as a database user on any database server, while web administrators have unlimited access to their servers. The backup lackeys can mount tapes and dump filesystems. Finally, the administrators can run anything they want. This sudoers is too simple to represent any real organization, but complex enough to illustrate transformations.

cvtsudoers Output Format

The cvtsudoers program can produce three different types of output: JSON, LDIF, and sudoers. The default is LDIF. Use the -f flag to set a different output format.

```
$ cvtsudoers /etc/global-sudoers -f sudoers
Defaults noexec, env_keep+=SSH_*
Defaults command_timeout=10
Defaults!SHELL command_timeout=2m
...
```

We're transforming the sudoers file into another sudoers file. It's not identical to the original sudoers, however. The comments are gone, and any included files are integrated to the file.

Rather than dumping the file to your terminal and redirecting, specify an output file with -o.

```
$ cvtsudoers /etc/sudoers -f sudoers -o complete-sudoers
```

If you want to see how sudo interprets your elegant multi-file policy, and how you messed it up, this is how.

We'll use sudoers format in this chapter, and LDIF in Chapter 11, but why does sudoers include JSON? Some people use JSON format for audits, but there are no publicly available JSON-based sudoers audit tools. Yet.

Filtering by Host, User, or Group

The sudoers file contains information about web servers and database servers. The organization security officer would really prefer that the web servers don't have any rules for the database servers, and contrariwise on the database servers. Use cvtsudoers to strip down the sudoers policy down to the rules that apply to a single host. You can filter based on host, user, or group with the –m option. While it's certainly useful to see "what sudo policy does `mike` have?" we're focusing on per-host filters. Here I pull the sudoers policy that applies to `www1`.

```
$ cvtsudoers -f sudoers -m host=www1 /etc/global-sudoers
Defaults noexec, env_keep+=SSH_*
Defaults command_timeout=10
Defaults!SHELL command_timeout=2m
Defaults!/usr/bin/visudo command_timeout=5m

Cmnd_Alias BACKUP = /sbin/dump, /sbin/restore, \
    /usr/bin/mt
Cmnd_Alias MAYEXEC = /usr/bin/newaliases, \
    /usr/local/sbin/visudo
Cmnd_Alias SHELL = /bin/sh, /bin/csh, /bin/tcsh, \
    /bin/bash, /usr/bin/su, /usr/local/bin/sudo
User_Alias TAPEMONKEYS = mike, pete, hank
Host_Alias WWW = www1, www2, www3
User_Alias WWWADMIN = adel, matt, nils
TAPEMONKEYS ALL = BACKUP

WWWADMIN WWW = ALL

%wheel ALL = (ALL) ALL
%wheel ALL = EXEC: MAYEXEC, SHELL
```

This policy is much the same as the original, but it has no mention of the database servers. Installing this on your web servers won't leak any information about the rest of your network.

You can match on a user alias or a host alias. Rather than matching on the single host `www1`, we could filter on all machines included in the WWW host alias.

```
$ cvtsudoers -f sudoers -m host=WWW /etc/global-sudoers
```

Separate multiple matches with a comma. Maybe Thea suspects me of shenanigans, and wants to see what privileges I have on the web servers.

Chapter 10: Policy Distribution

```
$ cvtsudoers -f sudoers -m host=WWW,user=mike global-sudoers
Defaults noexec, env_keep+=SSH_*
Defaults command_timeout=10
Defaults!SHELL command_timeout=2m
Defaults!/usr/bin/visudo command_timeout=5m
Defaults@thea !noexec, command_timeout=4h

Cmnd_Alias BACKUP = /sbin/dump, /sbin/restore, /usr/bin/mt
Cmnd_Alias SHELL = /bin/sh, /bin/csh, /bin/tcsh, /bin/bash, \
    /usr/bin/su,/usr/local/bin/sudo
User_Alias TAPEMONKEYS = mike, pete, hank

TAPEMONKEYS ALL = BACKUP
```

When filtering a policy, cvtsudoers ignores the local system's user and group databases. This means that if you have a user who's in **wheel**, cvtsudoers won't pick up that rule for users in that group. Add the -M flag to call on the system user database to perform such checks.

```
$ cvtsudoers -f sudoers -M host=WWW,user=mike global-sudoers
...
TAPEMONKEYS ALL = BACKUP
```

%wheel ALL = (ALL) ALL

%wheel ALL = EXEC: MAYEXEC, SHELL

Adding the -M here showed two more policy statements, because **mike** is in **wheel** on this host.[21] The local machine might not have the same users or groups as the machine this policy should be run on, though. Use -M or not, depending on your environment.

Depending on how your policy is written, it's possible that a filtered policy will include extraneous stuff. The -p flag filters most of that out.

Expanding Aliases

While aliases are convenient, sometimes you want to see the full rule as sudo will interpret it. The -e flag expands all aliases. Here I show the rules for the hosts in the WWW host alias.

---

21 I swear, I have no idea how my account got in wheel on this critical system. Computers do weird stuff sometimes, you know?

```
# cvtsudoers /etc/global-sudoers -e -m host=WWW
Defaults noexec, env_keep+=SSH_*
…
mike, pete, hank ALL = /sbin/dump, /sbin/restore, \
    /usr/bin/mt
%wheel ALL = (ALL) ALL
%wheel ALL = EXEC: /usr/bin/newaliases, \
    /usr/local/sbin/visudo, /bin/sh, /bin/csh, \
    /bin/tcsh, /bin/bash, /usr/bin/su, \
    /usr/local/bin/sudo
```

One advantage of this format is it lets you easily see that dubious ALL command alias, and eliminate it.

The cvtsudoers Config File

If you'll be repeatedly transforming your policy, consider setting options in the cvtsudoers configuration file, */etc/cvtsudoers.conf* or */usr/local/etc/cvtsudoers.conf*. Command line options override the configuration file, but this is a good way to set defaults. Set the value of each parameter with a space, an equals sign, and the value. Not including the spaces around the equals sign causes an error.

Suppose you only want to see output in sudoers format. Use the *output_format* parameter.

```
output_format = sudoers
```

You can now drop `-f sudoers` from your command line.

You can also specify a *match* condition in *cvtsudoers.conf*.

```
match = host=www1
```

This is fairly unique, and you wouldn't want to use it all the time. But cvtsudoers lets you use an alternate configuration file. That filter Thea wrote to catch my rules? She could create */etc/cvtsudoers.mike* with all her settings for that search and point cvtsudoers at that file with the `-c` option.

```
$ cvtsudoers -c /etc/cvtsudoers.mike
```

Find a complete list of *cvtsudoers.conf* options in the cvtsudoers(1) man page. You'll also find a bunch of other options in there, allowing you to display or hide parts of the ruleset. Many of these options are most useful when dealing with LDAP. Let's climb that mountain next.

"Well, sir, I have a silly sudoers and I'd like to obtain an LDAP server to help me distribute it."

Chapter 11: Security Policies in LDAP

One problem with sudo is that it's normally configured on the host it manages. An intruder or a disaffected user who leverages his way into altering the sudoers file can gain extra privileges. Eliminate this risk by removing the sudoers policy from the machine.

The Lightweight Directory Access Protocol (LDAP) is the standard protocol for providing directory-style information across a network. Really, it's nothing more than a database optimized for reads. The most common use for LDAP is verifying usernames and passwords across the enterprise, but it can support any arbitrary directory—including a sudo policy.

Migrating your sudoers policy to LDAP has several advantages. A user who compromises a host cannot alter the sudoers policy. Even gaining root on a server doesn't grant access to changing the read-only LDAP policy. Also, changes to an LDAP-based policy immediately propagate to all the machines on the network. LDAP servers reject improperly formatted data. You can mistype host and user names, but any sudo configuration the LDAP server accepts is syntactically valid. A busted sudoers distributed to all your machines won't prevent repairing the policy.

The disadvantages of configuring sudo from LDAP? First, you must have an LDAP server. When that LDAP server fails, your authentication and sudo policy die with it, so you probably want more than one. Each host must be integrated into LDAP. Most sudo installs lack LDAP support; you must find LDAP-aware sudo packages for your operating system.

Sudo includes very detailed documentation on providing a policy via LDAP in the `README.LDAP` included with the source code and the sudoers.ldap(5) man page. Both documents are also available on the sudo web site at https://sudo.ws. Read those documents before planning your deployment. This book does not replace the official sudo documentation; rather it provides context, guidance, and an overview parallel to that documentation. I don't cover details like AIX using `/etc/netsvc.conf` instead of `/etc/nsswitch.conf`; you must be familiar with how your operating system handles LDAP before even trying this.

Prerequisites

This is not a book on LDAP. If you don't know what a schema or an LDIF is, this section will baffle, annoy, and possibly scare you. That's because LDAP baffles, annoys, and scares the uninitiated. Skip to the next chapter. Logging sudo activity is much more interesting and useful than it sounds, and you don't need any external infrastructure to do it. This chapter focuses on LDAP-based sudo policies and attaching the sudo client to LDAP.

Involve your LDAP administrator in your planning before changing any configuration files or installing any software. LDAP might frustrate you, but your LDAP administrator spends a huge chunk of time maintaining that directory and keeping it pristine, or at least mostly functional. Early discussions, perhaps accompanied by small bribes, will smooth the whole project.

You must have LDAP-based authentication already working in a stable and secure manner. You need the ability to import LDIF files and make minor changes through an LDAP browser. I assume that you're using the same LDAP servers for sudo as for authentication. The LDAP sudo policy must not be writable by the clients it serves—otherwise, one compromised machine could alter the policy for the whole network.

If you don't have fully functional LDAP-based authentication, *stop*. You've gotten ahead of yourself. Get your machines pulling their users and groups from LDAP, and authenticating against that information. Then return here and try again.

I also assume that you're starting with a sudoers-based policy. It doesn't need to be a big policy—even something simple like "Here are some defaults, and this group gets full access" will get you rolling.

Site requirements vary too much for me to take you through a generic LDAP configuration. As OpenLDAP is the server most commonly used for sudo, I'll use it for specific detailed examples, but I'll also touch on Active Directory.

If all this hasn't sufficed to scare you off, you also need an LDAP-aware sudo and to teach the LDAP server to recognize sudo data.

An LDAP-aware sudo program works without a sudo policy in LDAP, so installing the version of sudo that speaks LDAP is a good place to start. Most operating systems have a sudo package built with LDAP support or allow you to easily enable it. Debian-based systems have a sudo-ldap package. On operating systems related to CentOS, enable LDAP in `/etc/nsswitch.conf`. FreeBSD users must build a custom sudo, but poudriere simplifies packaging and distributing it. Check your operating system documentation, and follow the instructions to get an LDAP-aware sudo on your system.

Then configure the LDAP server to recognize and serve that data.

The Sudo Schema

An LDAP server must understand the format and context of all its data. The data formatting specification is called a *schema*. Each vendor's LDAP server product has its own schema system that is subtly incompatible with all the other LDAP servers.[22] Sudo includes a few LDAP schemas, but the three that are most relevant are *schema.ActiveDirectory* (for Microsoft servers), *schema.OpenLDAP* (for traditional OpenLDAP servers), and *schema.olcSudo* (for OpenLDAP servers using the new online configuration).

Be sure to index the sudoUser attribute when adding the schema to your LDAP server.

Adding Sudo to Traditional OpenLDAP

To add the sudo schema to OpenLDAP, copy the OpenLDAP schema file to *sudo.schema* into your schema directory—probably */etc/openldap/schema/* or */usr/local/etc/openldap/schema/*. Then tell *slapd.conf* about the new schema, and add the *index* statement.

```
include /etc/openldap/schema/sudo.schema
index sudoUser eq
```

Restart slapd, and OpenLDAP will understand sudo policies.

OpenLDAP with Online Configuration

If you're using OpenLDAP's modern online configuration system, add the schema to your directory with ldapadd(1). Your LDAP administrator will know the exact command to communicate with your particular OpenLDAP configuration, but the following is not uncommon and is what I use to connect to my server **ldap1**.

```
# ldapadd -c -f schema.olcSudo -H ldap://ldap1 -W -x \
  -D cn=Manager,dc=mwl,dc=io
```

The new schema is immediately available.

---

22 Because LDAP vendors hate all that is wholesome.

Adding Sudo to Active Directory

Copy the `schema.ActiveDirectory` file to a domain controller and run the following command.
```
C:> ldifde -i -f schema.ActiveDirectory -c dc=X dc=mwl,dc=io
```
That's it.

The Policy Container

The sudo policy needs a home, or *container*, in the directory. A bunch of software is cranky about where its container must be placed, and juggling conflicting requirements imposed by different vendors makes LDAP administrators even more cranky. Sudo doesn't care where its container is, only that it has one. It defaults to using `ou=SUDOers, dc=example, dc=com` on OpenLDAP and `cn=sudoers, cn=Configuration, dc=example, dc=com` on Active Directory, but if that doesn't work for the LDAP administrator obey her wishes. LDAP causes her enough grief, she doesn't need any lip from you.

Here's an LDIF for a sudo container for the OpenLDAP server for **mwl.io**. For other servers or other container locations, change the Distinguished Name path.

```
dn: ou=SUDOers,dc=mwl,dc=io
objectClass: top
objectClass: organizationalUnit
ou: SUDOers
```

Import this into your directory, either at the command line or in your LDAP browser. Now create your initial sudo policy.

LDAP Sudo Policies versus Sudoers

Building a sudo security policy to be distributed via LDAP is different than creating a sudoers-based policy. It's different enough that "sudoers" specifically refers to a policy implemented via a *sudoers* file. You can't have sudoers in LDAP; you have a sudo policy in LDAP or an LDAP sudo policy.

First off, LDAP sudo policies do not support aliases. The user aliases, command aliases, and so forth that took up an earlier chapter of this book? Not applicable to LDAP sudo policies. Use LDAP groups for servers and users. This isn't necessarily an advantage or disadvantage, merely a difference. The design of LDAP means it's very easy to add a new command, user, or host to a rule, however.

A sudoers policy works on a "last match" basis, so you put generic rules at the top of the policy and get more specific further on. LDAP doesn't automatically deliver query results in deterministic order. You can order individual sudo rules in LDAP with the sudoOrder attribute, placing one rule before another so that "last match" works, but it's an extra step that demands mindfulness. You cannot order attributes within a single LDAP sudo policy statement.

Avoid using ALL for hosts as well as for commands. Create a list that contains all legitimate hosts and use that instead.

Multiple attributes are not supported in a single sudo policy statement. A complex sudoers policy statement will get split into multiple LDAP objects.

Unix groups are not the same as LDAP groups. If you want your policy to refer to the **wheel** group, you must create an LDAP **wheel** group.

Finally, LDAP sudo policies don't support negations for hosts, users, or RunAs statements. You can use negation for commands, but negating ALL is still easily evadable. You cannot order attributes within a policy rule, though, so any command negation takes precedence. Save yourself the indigestion, and don't try to use negations with LDAP sudo policies.

The easiest way to see how well your sudoers converts to LDAP? Run the converter and fix the errors.

Transforming Sudoers to LDIF

Chapter 10 discussed cvtsudoers, sudo's policy transformation tool. It was originally written to transform sudoers policies into LDAP policies. Before trying to run the conversion, though, get the location of the sudoers container from your LDAP administrator. You can give the location on the command line with the -b flag, but this is one case where setting an option in the configuration file is overwhelmingly preferable. Set the location in `cvtsudoers.conf` with the *sudoers_base* option. My container is at ou=SUDOers,dc=mwl,dc=io, so I would set it like this.

```
sudoers_base = ou=SUDOers,dc=mwl,dc=io
```

Remember, you must have a space around the first equals sign.

Once you have this set, converting your sudoers to LDIF requires only the file name. I'm using the same policy shown in our initial discussion of cvtsudoers at the end of Chapter 10. It's a long policy, so I'm not going to reprint it here. The -I option sets an increment for sudoOrder, while -O sets a starting point for sudoOrder. I set these to 100 for my small policy, but if you have a large complex policy you should probably increase these to 1000 or more. We'll discuss the them when discussing sudoOrder later this chapter.

```
$ cvtsudoers -I 100 -O 100 /etc/global-sudoers
```

Congratulations, you've done your first conversion! Except for everything that works in sudoers but not in LDAP, of course. Conveniently, cvtsudoers puts the list of problems right up front.

```
# Unable to translate /etc/global-sudoers:4
# Defaults!/bin/sh, /bin/csh, /bin/tcsh, /bin/bash, /usr/bin/su, /usr/local/bin/sudo command_timeout=2m

# Unable to translate /etc/global-sudoers:5
# Defaults!/usr/bin/visudo command_timeout=5m
…
```

Chapter 11: Security Policies in LDAP

Looking at the sample policy, the global default setting *command_timeout* to 10 worked fine. These lines failed to convert:

```
Defaults!SHELL command_timeout=2m
Defaults!/usr/bin/visudo command_timeout=5m
Defaults@thea !noexec, command_timeout=4h
```

We must convert these per-user, per-host, per-Run-As, and per-command defaults to use tags rather than options. This requires thinking about how the defaults get used in the policy.

This policy uses the *command_timeout* option to set running time limits for certain commands and users. The TIMEOUT tag works exactly like *command_timeout*, but applies to the privileges rather than defaults. These non-default options really come into play on the last few privileges.

```
%wheel            ALL = (ALL) ALL
%wheel            ALL = EXEC:MAYEXEC,SHELL
```

Turn back to the sample policy in Chapter 10 and think for a moment about what it's trying to accomplish. This policy says "anyone in wheel can run anything, but those programs can't run other programs. Only the programs listed in the MAYEXEC and SHELL aliases can run programs." The *command_timeout* option terminates all commands after 10 seconds. Visudo can run for five minutes and shells for two minutes. Thea can run any command for up to four hours.

Replicating this policy in pure privilege statements requires more rules.

```
%wheel            ALL = (ALL) ALL
%wheel            ALL = EXEC:MAYEXEC
%wheel            ALL = TIMEOUT=5m EXEC:/usr/bin/visudo
%wheel            ALL = TIMEOUT=2m EXEC:SHELL
thea              ALL = TIMEOUT=4h EXEC: ALL
```

This shows why we like Defaults. In sudoers, the effective policy is an intersection of Defaults and privilege rules. When using LDAP, however, everything must be expressed in privilege rules. The policy gets longer.

Run this through cvtsudoers again, and let's look at the results.

Sudo Rules in LDIF

The new LDIF file starts with a stanza representing a single directory entry.

```
dn: cn=defaults,ou=SUDOers,dc=mwl,dc=io
objectClass: top
objectClass: sudoRole
cn: defaults
description: Default sudoOption's go here
sudoOption: noexec
sudoOption: env_keep+=SSH_*
sudoOption: command_timeout=10
```

According to the first line, this object is named *defaults* and lives in my directory's SUDOers container. The ObjectClass lines attach this object to a sudo policy. The description was added by cvtsudoers, and tells us that this object contains all of the policy's global default settings. We then have three sudoOption statements, each giving a default option: *noexec*, *env_keep*, and *command_timeout*.

Look back at the original policy.

```
Defaults noexec, env_keep += "SSH_*"
Defaults command_timeout=10
```

Both of these lines can go into one LDAP object. The only reason to separate them in sudoers is because I like nice short lines.

If you skip past the aliases in the sample sudoers policy, you'll find a rule allowing people in the TAPEMONKEYS alias to run backup jobs. Here's that rule in LDIF.

```
dn: cn=TAPEMONKEYS,ou=SUDOers,dc=mwl,dc=io
objectClass: top
objectClass: sudoRole
cn: TAPEMONKEYS
sudoUser: mike
sudoUser: pete
sudoUser: hank
sudoHost: ALL
sudoCommand: /sbin/dump
sudoCommand: /sbin/restore
sudoCommand: /usr/bin/mt
sudoOrder: 100
```

The rule is named TAPEMONKEYS, after the alias, but lists the members of that alias as individual sudoUsers. The sudoHost entry says this applies to ALL hosts. Each command they're allowed to use is a separate sudoCommand. The conversion from sudoers to LDIF expanded all the aliases. The sudoOrder entry is the order of this rule inside the policy, allowing you to order your rules so that the last match behavior still works.

Let's plunge deeper into the various components of a sudo LDIF. I promise, it only hurts for a moment.

Sudo Rules and Roles

A one-line sudoers policy becomes a single LDAP entry, called a *sudoRole*. Both of the LDIF stanzas we considered in the previous section are sudoRoles.

All sudo attributes have limited permitted values. You can only put usernames in a username, or commands in a command. You cannot enter an invalid data type into an attribute—the space for a username won't accept an IP address, and the LDAP server will refuse the entry if you try. Mind you, an LDAP server has no way to know if "mike" is a username or a hostname, so you still need to verify that the syntactically-valid rule you wrote is correct. The one special value is ALL, which matches all possible entries for that attribute.

The value of a sudoUser attribute maps to the *uid* attribute in the user's posixUser object. Putting % before a sudoUser value tells LDAP to map the group to the *cn* attribute of a posixGroup object.

All sudoRoles have the Distinguished Name (DN) and Common Name (CN) attributes, as well as the sudoRole objectClass attribute. But three additional attributes must appear in every sudoRole, and a few more attributes can be useful. (We'll discuss sudoNotAfter and sudoNotBefore in Chapter 13.)

sudoUser

The sudoUser attribute is a user name, exactly like those in a sudoers policy. Remember, you cannot use aliases in a sudoUser attribute. You can use operating system groups, group IDs, and netgroups. Groups stored in LDAP work just fine. Each user name must appear in its own sudoUser entry within a sudoRole.

```
sudoUser: fred
sudoUser: kate
sudoUser: %wheel
```

This sudoRole applies to the users **fred** and **kate**, as well as everyone in the LDAP group **wheel**.

sudoHost

This is a list of hosts that this sudoRole applies to. Enter hosts using the same syntax and restrictions as a host list in a sudoers policy. You can use hostnames, IP addresses, networks, and netgroups.

```
sudoHost: 192.0.2.0/24
sudoHost: www.mwl.io
sudoHost: +office
```

The sudoHost attribute accepts negations. Put an exclamation point in front of the excluded host.

```
sudoHost: 198.51.100.0/24
sudoHost: !198.51.100.1
```

This sudoRole applies to all hosts with an IP from 198.51.100.2 through 198.51.100.254.

sudoCommand

This is the full path to a command, plus any command-line arguments and wild cards. This is exactly like the command list in sudoers, except that you cannot use sudoers aliases. ALL, just as in sudoers, matches all commands and is a really bad idea to combine with root privileges.

Use the word *sudoedit* followed by a file path to permit the user to edit the file with sudo, as discussed in Chapter 5. Similarly, putting a digest before the command tells sudo to verify the digest before executing the command.

```
sudoCommand:  /sbin/dump
sudoCommand:  sudoedit /etc/namedb/named.conf
sudoCommand:  sha512:fa73…091c /usr/bin/passwd
```

You can use negations in sudoCommand statements. They work exactly like command negations in sudoers. Never try to exclude commands from ALL.

In addition to the three mandatory attributes, LDAP-based policies have four optional components: sudoOption, sudoRunAsUser, sudoRunAsGroup, and sudoOrder.

sudoOption

This is a list of sudoers-style options that apply to this specific sudoRole. You can use sudoOption to override global defaults. Consider this LDIF snippet.

```
...
sudoCommand: /usr/bin/visudo
sudoOption: command_timeout=300
sudoOption: !noexec
...
```

When using the command `/usr/bin/visudo`, the option *command_timeout* is set to 300 and *noexec* is disabled. These override any global defaults.

sudoRunAsUser

The sudoRunAsUser attribute gives a list of target users that sudo users can run commands as. This works exactly like the RunAs list discussed in Chapter 4. The word ALL matches all users. The sudoRunAsUser attribute accepts user lists including usernames, user ID numbers, groups, and netgroups using the same syntax as a RunAs list.

```
sudoRunAsUser: pg
sudoRunAsUser: mysql
```

This sudoRole permits running commands as the database user.

sudoRunAsGroup

This attribute allows users to run commands as a member of a Unix group. The groups have the same valid names as groups within a sudoers policy.

```
sudoRunAsGroup: operator
```

Most often, however, you want to run commands as another user rather than a group member.

sudoOrder

This attribute allows you to assign rule order. Roles are processed in order, from lowest to highest. The sudoOrder attribute lets you emulate the last matching rule behavior from the sudoers policy. A sudoRole without a sudoOrder has an order of 0, and so is processed first. If you have multiple sudoRoles without a sudoOrder, they are processed in random order. The maximum value is the size of a signed double, which is over 2.8×10^{78} (1.79769^{308}) on almost all modern hardware.

Each sudoRole can have only one sudoOrder.

During the conversion from sudoers to LDIF, I used the -I 100 and -O 100 flags to cvtsudoers. This started numbering sudoRoles with 100, and incremented sudoOrder by 100 with each new sudoRole. This gives you space to add new sudoRole statements between existing rules. If you have a large policy, consider increments of 1,000 or 10,000.

Some huge organizations allocate sudoOrder by blocks. Rules 1 through 1000 might be locally set, while 2000 through 3000 might be regional, 4000 through 5000 global, and so on. Use -I and -O to assign the appropriate ranges to the generated LDAP objects.

Activating LDAP in sudo(8)

Now that you have a sudo policy in LDAP, point a client at it. Your sudo binary might be linked against the LDAP libraries, but it certainly won't search LDAP by default. You must tell sudo where to find the SUDOers LDAP container, then configure sudo to use that policy.

Finding the LDAP Policy

Every Unix vendor and distributor has integrated LDAP support in the manner they believe most correct, and lives in eternal hope that all the other vendors will experience an epiphany and join them in obvious technological superiority.[23] Until that glorious day, however, every Unix configures LDAP slightly differently. I said earlier than you must have a working LDAP setup, where your host can pull user, group, and

---

23   This is possible, but the odds are roughly equivalent to the chances of me deciding to work sales engineering for Oracle.

authentication information from your LDAP directory. The reason this is vital is because it means you already know what weird settings your Unix needs to talk to the directory, and can piggyback on that knowledge to configure sudo.

While sudo can be compiled against any number of LDAP libraries, it always uses OpenLDAP-style syntax.

Start by running `sudo -V` to ask your sudo install where it expects to find its LDAP configuration.

```
# sudo -V | grep -i ^ldap
ldap.conf path: /etc/ldap.conf
ldap.secret path: /etc/ldap.secret
```

This particular sudo install expects to find `ldap.conf` and `ldap.secret` in `/etc`, the default for this operating system. (Set different locations with the *ldap_conf* and *ldap_secret* options to the sudoers policy plugin in `sudo.conf`, as discussed in Chapter 7.)

Most (but not all) operating systems can share a single `ldap.conf` between all LDAP-aware applications. This means you can add a couple of lines to your configuration and get sudo working. Others use sudo-specific LDAP configurations, however. For those, you can usually copy the standard `ldap.conf` to the sudo-specific `ldap.conf` and proceed from there. Check your operating system manual if you have any concerns.[24]

Add the sudo LDAP configuration to whichever `ldap.conf` sudo reads. While sudo reads all of the standard OpenLDAP variables to connect to the LDAP server, it has three sudo-specific configuration values: *sudoers_base*, *sudoers_search_filter*, and *sudoers_timed*. We discuss *sudoers_timed* in Chapter 13.

---

24 A couple distributions required blood sacrifices at the second dark of the moon in a month to make sudo read its policy from LDAP, but I'm assured that this behavior was corrected once enough users filed sufficiently detailed bug reports. On most distributions, at least.

The *sudoers_base* value gives the location of the sudo policy container. If you have multiple *sudoers_base* entries, sudo will query them in order. The standard *sudoers_base* on my network looks like this.

```
sudoers_base ou=sudoers,dc=mwl,dc=io
```

This configuration suffices to access the policy.

The *sudoers_search_filter* parameter lets you give an LDAP search filter to reduce the number of results returned by the LDAP query. Sudo works fine without this filter; if you need one, your LDAP administrator will inform you.

Old documentation mentions *sudoers_debug*, but this is deprecated and due to be buried in an unmarked grave any time now. Use the logging discussed in Chapter 12 instead.

Now that your LDAP clients can find the policy, tell sudo to use it.

Tell sudo To Use LDAP

Almost every Unix uses `/etc/nsswitch.conf` to tell programs where to get information. The most commonly configured resources are hostnames and usernames, but sudo uses it as well. Standard sudo has two possible policy sources, *ldap* and *files*. (We'll discuss *sssd* later this chapter.) List them in the order you want them used.

```
sudoers: ldap files
```

If your sudo install should never use the local sudoers file, remove *files* from the list. That's not quite enough to disable sudoers, however.

Disabling Sudoers

To tell sudo to completely ignore the sudoers file, use the *ignore_local_sudoers* option in your LDAP policy. Put it in your default settings.

```
dn: cn=defaults,ou=SUDOers,dc=mwl,dc=io
objectClass: top
objectClass: sudoRole
cn: defaults
description: Default sudoOption's go here
sudoOption: noexec
sudoOption: env_keep+=SSH_*
sudoOption: command_timeout=10
sudoOption: ignore_local_sudoers
...
```

When sudo sees this option in LDAP, it never looks at the sudoers file.

The question is, do you *want* to disable local sudoers policies? Probably. An LDAP client without LDAP is crippled at best. In case of disaster, I often put an empty sudoers file on my LDAP clients, and mark it as inaccessible using filesystem flags or ACLs.

Migrations and Learning SudoRoles

Once you have your first hosts reading their sudo policies from LDAP, don't instantly deploy LDAPilated sudo across your network. Yes, that first warm rush of victory against sudo and LDAP feels pretty good, but hurried deployments cause pain.[25] Thoroughly test your sudo policy on those first hosts. Verify that everyone has the access they need and, just as important, doesn't have extra access. If you have hundreds of web servers, implement on one or two before flipping the switch on the whole farm. Repeat the process for your database servers, file servers, and so on.

If managing LDAP isn't your job, but you want to support sudo policies via LDAP, congratulations! You get to learn a new skill! Once you understand writing sudoers policies, though, expressing the same thing in LDAP isn't that much harder.

---

25   Sysadmin rule #6: Deploy in haste, repent in leisure.

If you get confused, cvtsudoers is your friend. If you don't know how to write a policy in LDIF, write a sudoers entry for that policy and convert that to LDIF. Modifying that LDIF is much easier than writing one from scratch. Soon, you'll be writing and editing sudoRole LDIFs effortlessly. Don't tell the LDAP administrator that you can write LDIFs, however, or she might suck you into writing more of them.

Some people write their policies in sudoers, then use cvtsudoers to convert the policy into LDIF and replace the whole SUDOers container. While technically acceptable, this approach lacks elegance. If you're not familiar with LDAP but have the responsibility for maintaining a complex sudo policy, auditing an LDAP sudo policy will not appeal. Fortunately, migrating the policy into LDAP is not a one-way journey. Have your LDAP administrator teach you how to export the SUDOers container as an LDIF, then use cvtsudoers to transform that LDIF into the more familiar sudoers format. Use -f to set cvtsudoers' output format, and -i to set the input format.

```
$ cvtsudoers -f sudoers -i ldif SUDOers-ldif
```

While reviewing the policy in its more familiar form, be sure to match the individual rules to the LDAP entries. It's the only way you'll become comfortable with LDAP sudo.

LDAP Caching

The biggest risk when using LDAP for authentication and policy distribution is that your network becomes dependent on the LDAP servers. Hopefully you have multiple LDAP servers, distributed in such a way that they resist most failure scenarios. And hopefully you have sufficient LDAP servers that the loss of a substantial fraction of them won't overload the survivors.

You can cache LDAP information locally on each machine, to tide the servers through a brief outage. Programs like the System Security

Services Daemon (SSSD) and the Name Service Caching Daemon (NSCD) can cache LDAP lookups, but sudo has specific support for SSSD. The details of implementing SSSD vary enough between operating systems that I can't cover it here, but the sudo part of the configuration is straightforward. If your sudo supports SSSD, add *sssd* as an information source in */etc/nsswitch.conf*.

```
sudo: sssd
```

This lets sudo reference the cached security policy even when the LDAP servers have failed. You can also configure SSSD to proactively download and cache the sudo policy from the LDAP server so that it's prepared for an LDAP failure.

Now let's consider sudo logging. It's more useful than you think.

"Nobody expects the Sudo Inquisition!"

Chapter 12: Logging, Mail, and Debugging

You now control which privileged commands people have access to. Everything's good, right? Certainly... until the day you find half of your servers hung because the `/usr` filesystems have fled for parts unknown. Everybody will want to know who to blame. Sudo has three different logging systems: a simple "what sudo did" syslog, a debugging log, and full session capture logs. (There's also a private sudo logfile, but it's a leftover from the 1980s and not widely used today.) Sudo can also notify the system owner or security team when folks use sudo.

Syslog

Sudo logs activity through the standard syslog protocol. On your average Unix host, sudo logs show up in a file like `/var/log/secure` or `/var/log/auth.log`. Here's a typical sudo log message.

```
Jul 12 12:07:28 www1 sudo[18118]:  mike : TTY=pts/0 ; PWD=/usr/home/mike ; USER=root ; COMMAND=/usr/bin/passwd pete
```

Sudo logs the date and time it was run, and the machine name (**www1**). Then there's the command name and PID, the user who ran sudo (**mike**), and the terminal it was run in (`pts/0`). Lastly we get the working directory (`/usr/home/mike`), the user the command was run as (**root**), and the command run via sudo (`/usr/bin/passwd pete`).

Sudo also logs when a user can't run a command.

```
Jul 12 12:15:29 freebsd sudo[26870]:  mike : command not allowed ; TTY=pts/0 ; PWD=/usr/home/mike ; USER=root ;
```

```
COMMAND=/usr/bin/passwd root
```

Note the string *command not allowed*. Looks like someone's trying to escape his cage. Again. The boss needs to have a word with him. Again.

Customizing Sudo Syslog

Sudo uses the *authpriv* log facility, dumping its logs in with other security-sensitive information like login and logout. If your Unix doesn't support *authpriv*, sudo falls back on *auth*. This is better than using the main system log, but still leaves a couple issues. Sudo success and failure messages alike get dumped into all the other authentication records. This makes searching the logs more complicated than necessary. Depending on the problem you're trying to troubleshoot or the audit report you must write, you'll care about either successes or failures. Only rarely will you want both simultaneously. Configure sudo to send logs to different facilities and priorities, and the set up syslogd to put those messages in separate files.

Set log facilities and levels in sudoers using the options *syslog*, *syslog_badpri*, and *syslog_goodpri*. What facilities and priorities should you choose? That depends entirely on what's available in your environment. If you want to also log which process ID ran sudo, set the *syslog_pid* option. Here I tell sudo to use the facility *LOCAL2*, log failures at *crit* priority, and log successes at *info*.

```
Defaults syslog=local2,syslog_badpri=crit,\
    syslog_goodpri=info
```

Now tell syslogd to split out this facility and each priority into its own logfile. Here's how you would do this in `syslog.conf` on a host running traditional syslogd.

```
local2.=crit    /var/log/sudofail
local2.=info    /var/log/sudo
```

Some syslog implementations restrict log message length. If you trip over this limit, set the *syslog_maxlen* option in sudoers to tell sudo to split long messages at a certain number of bytes.

Reading the sudo logs open up interesting customer service possibilities. Repeated sudo failures indicate either that someone *has* a problem, or someone *is* a problem. Either a user is testing their limits, or they're trying to do their job but failing, or they're flailing around helplessly in the desperate hope that the instructions in a HOWTO old enough to have a medical license will somehow work this time. When a helpdesk flunky has a little spare time, they can pick up the phone and say "Hey, we see that you're having trouble." The end user will feel supported or watched. Either way, a touch of omniscience never hurts your reputation.

Syslog Security

Syslog doesn't have the greatest reputation for security. Most syslog installations write their logs to the local host. A privileged but malicious user can edit those logs to hide evidence of their malfeasance. They don't even need a shell. A privileged user willing to wield sed(1) and awk(1) with malice aforethought can do terrible things to your innocent servers.

The only way around this is to have syslog send all messages to a remote logging host. While any number of network problems can disrupt message delivery, it's better than leaving everything on only the local host. This `syslog.conf` entry sends all messages to the host **loghost**.

```
*.*     @loghost
```

If you can't send all the system logs, at least send the sudo logs.

```
local2.=crit    /var/log/sudofail,@loghost
local2.=info    /var/log/sudo,@loghost
```

Use a syslog daemon that securely transmits messages to your logging host. Most traditional syslogs, as well as newer ones like syslog-ng and rsyslogd, now support TCP and TLS.

Email

Chances are you've seen emails from sudo, complaining that someone tried to use it and failed. You can adjust which events sudo sends email about, who sudo sends that email to, or whether it notifies anyone at all. These notifications can quickly alert you when a user is having trouble, and can help you notice intrusions—if your web server user starts trying to run sudo, you have a problem. In a large environment, though, those emails are nothing but a distraction.

Many sudo installs email `root` whenever a user has any problem. It doesn't matter if they can't authenticate or don't have the rights to run or if they flat-out aren't listed in the security policy. If nobody reads emails addressed to `root`, those emails will pile up until they fill the partition. Either forward sudo (and `root`!) emails to an account where someone will read them, or disable them.

Sudo relies on the host's email system to send mail. If the host doesn't have working email, sudo can't send mail.

Sudo does not send mail when people run `sudo -l` or `sudo -V`. Users are allowed to query their permissions or check the sudo version without attracting the sysadmin's notice.

Sending Mail

You can control who sudo sends email to, the account it's sent from, and the subject of the email.

Set the recipient with the *mailto* option. Double-quote the recipient so sudo doesn't try to interpret the @ sign as a marker for a hostname. In this example, I'm sending mail to sudo@mwl.io. Set the mail subject with *mailsub*. Again, double-quote the subject line. Finally, set the mail's From address with the *mailfrom* option.

```
Defaults mailto="sudo@mwl.io"
Defaults mailsub="sudo annoyances"
Defaults mailfrom="sudo@mwl.io"
```

Once you have these set, decide when you want sudo to send you email.

Setting Email Conditions

Modern sudo sends no email notifications by default.

To get an email any time anyone uses sudo, successfully or not, enable the *mail_all_cmnds* option. You'll get an email of every success and failure. If you want an email only when someone successfully uses sudo, enable the *mail_always* option.

Sudo also supports notifications for more narrow cases. If you want to be notified when a user has permission to run a command but cannot authenticate, enable *mail_badpass*. To be notified when a user who's listed in sudoers tries to run a command on a host where he's not permitted to use sudo, enable *mail_no_host*. If you're interested in users who try to run commands that are not listed or are explicitly denied, enable *mail_no_perms*.

To be notified when a user who doesn't even appear in the policy tries to use sudo, enable *mail_no_user*.

Mail Tags

Use the MAIL and NOMAIL tags to fine-tune which commands trigger an email. Maybe you don't want notifications any time someone uses routine commands, but you want an email anyone fires up a full-on privileged command prompt. I've defined the command alias SHELLS earlier in my policy for all the commands that offer a privileged command prompt.

```
%wheel ALL = ALL
%wheel ALL = MAIL:SHELLS
```

Attach these tags to particular users or aliases to keep a careful eye on the new sysadmins or abused commands.

Debugging Sudo and Sudoers

Writing a sudoers policy is fairly straightforward. Running sudo(8) is easy. But when things don't work as expected, sudo can drive you to madness. While it's entirely conceivable that you've discovered a legitimate bug, the truth is you probably don't understand how sudo implements your policy.

Debugging lets you log sudo's behavior as it processes your commands and policy, showing exactly how sudo makes decisions and make adjustments to get what you want. Set up all sudo(8) debugging in `sudo.conf`.

Subsystems and Levels

Sudo debugging is modeled after syslog. Debugging messages are configured into *levels* and *subsystems*.

A level is a measure of severity or priority. Sudo's levels, from low to high, are *debug*, *trace*, *info*, *diag*, *notice*, *warn*, *err*, and *crit*. The *debug* level includes every trivial bit of information that passes through sudo, while *crit* only presents the most severe problems. Which level do you need? That depends on how much detail you want. I find that *notice* provides enough detail to identify most of my mistakes. Lower levels produce hundreds of lines of output even for simple commands, but are useful for bug reports. Like syslog, setting a sudo debugging level logs everything of the given priority or higher. If you choose to log *notice* events, *warn*, *err*, and *crit* come along for the ride.

In addition to severity levels, sudo debugs on a per-subsystem basis. You can debug activity from each subsystem separately. If sudoedit is giving you grief, specifically log sudoedit events. If sudo seems to match the wrong per-host rules, log network interface handling.

The sudo(8) man page lists every subsystem the sudo program itself supports, but here are the most useful ones for debugging the sudo front end. Configure them in `sudo.conf`.

all – every subsystem

edit – sudoedit

netif – network interface handling

selinux – SELinux interactions

The sudoers policy engine has its own subsystems. Configure these in the sudoers file. Again, see sudoers(5) for a complete list of subsystems; these are merely the ones I find myself using.

alias – processing all aliases

all – every subsystem

auth – user authentication

defaults – processing Defaults

env – environment handling

ldap – LDAP information

match – matching users, groups, hosts, and netgroups

netif – network interface handling

sssd – interactions with SSSD.

The visudo and sudoedit commands can also be debugged, but they have only one subsystem: *all*.

If you don't know what to log, start with a high level of *all* and trim down from there.

Configuring Debug Logging

Configure debugging logging with a *Debug* statement. This statement takes three arguments: the sudo component to be debugged, the debug file name, and the system and level to debug. Here I set a debugging log in `/var/log/sudo_debug`, and have it log absolutely everything about the sudo command.

```
Debug sudo /var/log/sudo_debug all@debug
```

If I put this in `sudo.conf`, a simple `sudo -l` generates 1,598 lines of output. Don't enable this lightly.

You can debug four components: sudo itself, sudoers, visudo, and sudoedit. To see why visudo is choking, you might try this.

```
Debug visudo /var/log/visudo_debug all@notice
```

If you don't get useful information, try increasing the debugging level until you see something intriguing.

Sudo can log different subsystems at different levels. If you are experimenting with sudo authentication, you might want to crank up authentication logging.

```
Debug sudo /var/log/sudo_debug all@notice,auth@debug
```

Each component can have only one Debug statement.

Debug Usefulness

Sudo has a whole bunch of subsystems. Some of them, like LDAP and environment handling, produce very useful debugging logs. Others, like the *main* subsystem for sudo's main program, produce output meaningful only to sudo developers. If you're trying to understand a weird sudo behavior and can't see anything useful in the log, increase the number of subsystems you're logging and/or the log level. Worst case, logging everything at the debug level will get you all the information sudo produces. After that, you'll have to fall back on truss and DTrace and the sudo-users mailing list.

Complete Session Logging

Sudo records each user's basic activity with syslog. You can debug sudo and send notifications about who's using sudo. But none of these record what people do within privileged commands. You might know that a user ran a privileged shell or gpart(8), but there's no record of what happened inside that session.

Enter the sudo I/O log and sudoreplay(8).

When sudo runs commands, it can see any input or output of that command. By logging and timestamping the input and output, it can later display that session exactly as it happened. As these logs consume a larger amount of disk space than syslog-style logs like `/var/log/secure`, you must configure them separately.

I/O Log Directory

Before enabling sudo logs, consider where you want to store these logs and what you want to happen when logging fails.

Just as with any other system stored on the local machine, sudo I/O logs are subject to tampering by a privileged user. The logs are in a fairly complex format, with multiple files stored in hierarchical directories, so while not tamper-resistant they're certainly tamper-annoying. An educated intruder or knowledgeable malicious user would certainly destroy this evidence. The only way to resist this tampering is to store the logs off the machine. Sudo I/O logs are not in syslog format, however. The only way to store them off the machine is to use a remote filesystem like NFS, and blocking your host from deleting files on that NFS share. That means using NFS version 4, and configuring NFSv4 ACLs. The specifics of configuring ACLs varies widely between Unixes, so I'm not going to give command line examples. The sudo I/O log filesystem needs the append-only ACL for the sudo client, and you must verify that the ACL propagates to newly created files and directories. As the NFSv4 ACL specification is four times the size of this book, I'm going to stop discussing them here.

If you use remote logging, don't mix logs from multiple hosts in one directory. Each host needs its own I/O log directory.

The I/O log is normally stored in `/var/log/sudo-io`. Change this with the *iolog_dir* option. You can configure the I/O log to store records in a variety of directories named after the invoking user and their primary group, RunAs users and groups, hostnames, and commands, but sudoreplay's search engine makes this kind of separation almost always unnecessary. Similarly, while the I/O logs can have a different owner and group for the log directory, it's generally unadvisable.

When logging is configured, sudo refuses to run if it can't log the session. A knowledgeable intruder will fry the logs and logging ability first thing, so this makes sense. But when NFS is down or your local disk is full, sudo won't work. Disable this behavior by setting *ignore_iolog_errors*, but this will put you in the position of knowing all the innocent activity, but not the malicious.

I strongly encourage not setting *ignore_iolog_errors*. If you need—not *want*, *need*—I/O logging, you must have a monitoring system that alerts you to filesystem problems before they become critical. Consider your failure paths before mandating this globally, however. Your NFS servers and packet filters probably need *ignore_iolog_errors* so you can repair the NFS service and restore connectivity to your clients.

Enabling I/O Logging

Enable I/O logging of everything that appears on the screen with the *log_output* option. Don't log the output from sudoreplay, as every time you view a session you'll duplicate the contents of the session you're viewing in a slightly larger log file. Similarly, don't log the contents of commands like reboot(8) or shutdown(8). These commands unmount the filesystems sudo tries to write to; nothing good will come of the attempt. You'll probably find a couple of other problem commands on any given Unix, so create an alias for these troublemakers.

```
Defaults log_output
Cmnd_Alias NOIOLOG = /usr/local/bin/sudoreplay, \
   /sbin/reboot, /sbin/shutdown
Defaults!NOIOLOG !log_output
```

Selectively enable logging with the *LOG_OUTPUT* tag, and disable it with the *NOLOG_OUTPUT* tag and the option *nolog_output* or *!log_output*. Use whichever method makes your policy more legible.

Sudo also supports the *log_input* option. Where *log_output* records everything that appears on the screen, *log_input* records everything that the user types. This includes passwords and other sensitive information, which are stored unencrypted in the I/O log. If you must log input for specific commands, consider applying the *LOG_INPUT* and *NOLOG_INPUT* tags.

Listing I/O Logs

View the list of saved sessions with sudoreplay(8). Enable I/O logging and your test machine and run a few sudo commands to create some logs. Then run `sudoreplay -l` as **root** to list those sessions.

```
% sudo sudoreplay -l
Password:
Jul 15 13:47:15 2019 : mike : TTY=/dev/pts/4 ; CWD=/usr/
home/mike ; USER=root ; TSID=000001 ; COMMAND=/bin/emacs
/etc/fstab
Jul 15 13:49:47 2019 : thea : TTY=/dev/pts/2 ; CWD=/var/
log ; USER=root ; TSID=000002 ; COMMAND=/bin/ls sudo-io/
Jul 15 14:38:17 2019 : mike : TTY=/dev/pts/5 ; CWD=/usr/
home/mike ; USER=root ; TSID=000003 ; COMMAND=/usr/bin/
passwd root
```

Each entry includes several fields, delimited by either colons or semicolons. The entry starts with a timestamp in the system's time zone. The first log entry was recorded at 13:47:15, or 1:47 PM, on 15 July 2019.

The next field is the account who ran the command—in the first entry `mike`, and the second, `thea`.

Then there's the terminal. Sudo runs logged sessions in a new pseudoterminal, allowing it to capture all this I/O.

The current working directory, CWD, is next. Editing the copy of `/etc/fstab` in your home directory is very different from editing the actual `/etc/fstab`, and this field lets you differentiate between the two.

The USER field identifies the user the command was run as. Here, both Thea and I ran a command as `root`.

The TSID the unique identifier for this I/O log. It's a 36-bit number (0-9 and A-Z) allowing a little over two billion I/O logs on one host. The TSIDs in our example look nice and simple, but after a while you'll get ones like A9QZ8L. When I/O logging is enabled, the TSID also gets written to the system log message.

At the end you'll see the command run under sudo. I ran `emacs /etc/fstab` on the first command, while Thea ran `ls sudo-io`. My command is the same everywhere, thanks to the absolute path, but you'll need to check the current working directory field to see that she was looking into the true `/var/log/sudo-io`. In the third, I ran `passwd root`. Sudo records all commands by full path.

Viewing Individual Sessions

To view a session, give sudoreplay the complete TSID of the session. Let's look at what happened in session 000003.

```
# sudoreplay 000003
Replaying sudo session: /usr/bin/passwd root
Changing local password for root
New Password:
Retype New Password:
Replay finished, press any key to restore the terminal.
```

Sudoreplay immediately resizes the terminal to match the size of the terminal in the original session. (This doesn't happen when using terminals that ignore standard X conventions, most notably KDE's konsole(1).) It then displays what happened in real time. If I paused a few seconds to type a password, the replay also pauses in that spot. There's no visible change because the terminal displayed no output as I typed the new password. At the end, we're prompted to hit a key to restore our terminal to its previous size.

While syslog might show that I ran passwd(1), with only that as evidence I could plausibly claim that I interrupted the command before completing the password change. The session log shows otherwise.

Altering Playback

The ability to play back sessions is useful, but sometimes a session runs too quickly to understand or too slowly to watch comfortably. Use the space bar to pause and resume the replay. A less than symbol (<) cuts replay speed in half, while the greater than symbol (>) doubles it.

Before starting the playback, sudoreplay's -m option sets a maximum number of seconds to pause between changes, either key presses or screen output. Maybe you logged the output of a complicated install process that took a long time to run, and you want to see each screen for only two seconds rather than the five minutes it actually took. Or maybe Thea knew from the first time she saw the replay that I spent a lot of time sitting at the password prompt when I illicitly changed the root password, and she wants to accelerate the display during yet another Human Resources meeting.[26]

```
# sudoreplay -m 1 000003
```

Use the -s option to change the speed of the entire replay. The replay speed is divided by the argument. If you use -s 4, the replay runs four times as fast. Use -s 0.25 to make the replay run at one-quarter speed.

---

[26] I'd probably be in my own HR meeting a little after, if I wasn't the owner's brother-in-law.

```
# sudoreplay -s0.25 00A9XL81
```

Between `-s`, `-m`, and the interactive controls, you can adjust replays as needed.

Real Time Monitoring

It's entirely possible to watch a sudo session in near real time via the I/O log. Sort of real time, at least. Within a few seconds, or at least a minute or so. Sudo compresses logs and relies on the filesystem to ensure they're saved, which slows log accessibility.

When you write a file to disk, the filesystem doesn't necessarily immediately flip the bits on the underlying storage medium. The most constrained resource in almost any computer is disk I/O, so filesystems arrange and buffer write requests to optimize that resource. Your sudo I/O is just another request among many. By setting the *iolog_flush* option, you tell sudo to request that its I/O logs not be buffered, but rather written immediately to disk. This doesn't guarantee success—most disks have some sort of hardware write cache that can still muck up the process. And demanding priority for getting data on the disk means de-prioritizing efficiency in how that data gets laid out.

The I/O logs' plain text files are highly compressible, and get gzipped into filesystem-friendly chunks by default. Immediately flushing the logs to disk significantly reduces compression. If you have a transparently compressing filesystem like ZFS, you might consider disabling the *compress_io* option and letting the filesystem handle compression for you.

Searching I/O Logs

Traditionally, you figured out who did what by running grep on the system logs. Sudoreplay lets you search the I/O log by user, command, working directory, Run As user or group, terminal, and date.

The *command* keyword searches for a command that matches your search term. (Strictly speaking, your search term is a POSIX regular expression.) Here Thea searches out the filthy Emacs users, like me.

sudoreplay -l command emacs

The *cwd* keyword searches for commands run in a given canonical directory. Don't include a trailing slash in the directory name. Also, the directory must exactly match—searching for */etc/* will not match */etc/ssh/*, and searching for */home/mike/* will not work if */home/* is really */usr/home/mike/*. And users can run commands from any directory. The value of *cwd* exists mostly for interpretation of other fields, but it exists so we can search it. Here's a search for all sudo runs in the */etc/* directory.

sudoreplay -l cwd /etc

To view all sudo sessions run by a specific user, give the *user* keyword and the account name.

$ **sudoreplay -l user mike**

The *group* keyword searches for commands run as a particular group. The user must have explicitly requested to run a command as this group with `sudo -g` for this filter to match.

To search for commands run as a specific user, use the *runas* keyword.

$ **sudoreplay -l runas mysql**

Search by terminal device with the *tty* keyword. This is mostly useless for remote sessions, but it's great for seeing what was done on the actual console.

$ **sudoreplay -l tty /dev/console**

Most often, we want to know what happened within a period of time. To search for all sudo usage on or after a given date, use the *fromdate* keyword. To view sudo usage before but not including a date, use the keyword *todate*. The trick comes in expressing the date. Sudoreplay lets you express dates in many ways, and I only cover the ones I find most useful here. Check the sudoreplay man page for the details—but any program that lets you search by fortnight contains more search options than I'm willing to make you read about. You must quote multi-word time formats.

Sudoreplay supports many vernacular expressions like "last week," "today," "4 hours ago," and so on. For queries that cover a day, sudoreplay assumes the day starts at midnight. Here I look for everything that's happened in the last hour.

```
# sudoreplay -l fromdate "1 hour ago"
```

Maybe I want everything that happened more recently than 12 hours ago, but not within the last hour.

```
# sudoreplay -l fromdate "12 hours ago" \
    todate "1 hour ago"
```

Specify exact dates and times with AM and PM. Here I search for what happened between 1PM and 2PM on the fifteenth of July of this year.

```
# sudoreplay -l fromdate "1pm 15 July" \
    todate "2pm 15 July"
```

Now ask for the same thing, but in a different year.

```
# sudoreplay -l fromdate "1pm 15 July 2013" \
    todate "2pm 15 July 2013"
```

When you use words for months, the day and month can appear in any order. If you use numerical months, the month must appear before the day. This next example searches any entries after 1 April.

```
# sudoreplay -l fromdate 4/1
```

Use `1/4` instead and you'll search 4 January instead. Name your months and you'll avoid this whole problem.[27]

You can combine search keywords beyond just dates. The example below searches for my account running passwd after the first of July.

```
# sudoreplay -l fromdate "1 July" user mike \
    command passwd
```

Combine searches with the *or* operator.

```
# sudoreplay -l command sh or command bash or command su
```

This should get you well on your way to searching I/O logs. I recommend not drinking anything when you first peruse what your users actually use sudo for, as a spit-take wastes good caffeine.

I/O Log Rotation

The I/O log rotates itself, until you run out of disk space.

A host can have a little over two billion TSIDs, so the logs are broken up into subdirectories of */var/log/sudo-io* based on the TSID. Each two characters of the TSID gets its own directory—that is, the records for TSID 1X00LY is stored in the subdirectory *1X/00/LY*. You can customize the log directory layout with the *iolog_dir* option, but it's rarely useful.

Almost nobody needs two billion history entries for a single host, except perhaps someone writing their PhD on evolving sysadmin practices. For many organizations, this kind of log retention is a serious liability. I schedule find(1) commands to remove all entries older than a specific number of days. Here I delete all records older than 365 days.

```
# find /var/log/sudo-io/ -type f -mtime +365 -delete -print
```

---

27   Any system that formats dates as month-day-year is wrong.

Put this script into the host's cron, and you'll get a daily email reporting what logs got deleted. You might also add a command to delete empty directories, but the specifics of how to do that efficiently vary from Unix to Unix.

If you have enough disk space to keep a complete history of TSIDs, and you don't care about possibly getting subpoenaed for ancient records, let them stay. Once sudo uses TSID ZZZZZZ, it overwrites TSID 000000. This is problematic if you're storing the logs on append-only media.

Now that you can record exactly what users do, let's customize how they get sudo access in the first place.

> *"Strange PAM modules lying in ponds distributing credentials is no basis for a system of authentication! Supreme executive power derives from two-factor authentication, not from some farcical password ceremony."*

Chapter 13: Authentication

Sudo's authentication system looks pretty straightforward: enter your password and run a privileged command. Sudo will let you change how it handles passwords, how often users must enter their passwords, and if it even accepts passwords. You can tell sudo to demand authentication via a hardware token or SSH agent or some other authentication method I've never even heard of, and how it handles that authentication method.

We'll start by fine-tuning password management and then head into progressively stranger territory.

Password Management and Failure

You can dictate how sudo requests passwords, how many times sudo lets a user try to enter a password, and how sudo responds to incorrect passwords.

Password Attempts and Timeouts

Sudo gives users three chances to enter their password before giving up on them. Maybe your users can't successfully type their passwords on that first, second, or even third try. Use the *password_tries* option to give them a different number of attempts. Setting *passwd_tries* to 0 disables any attempt to authenticate.

Similarly, sudo gives a user five minutes to type their password before timing out the command. Personally, I find this excessive—if a user can't type their password in sixty seconds, I don't want them on my server. Use the *passwd_timeout* option to set a timeout in minutes. If any password attempt sits idle for this long, sudo exits.

Here each user is allowed five attempts to get their password right, and has two minutes to complete typing their password.

```
Defaults passwd_tries=5, passwd_timeout=2
```

You can set these options on a per-user basis. The owner of the company I work for often comes in groggy and trembling after a night stuffed with spectacular oligarchic debauchery, and none of us can keep him in line. He gets extra chances to enter his password and no timeout.[28]

```
Defaults:chad passwd_tries=100,passwd_timeout=0
```

Sudo normally offers no feedback when a user enters a password. If you want the user to get visual feedback when they type, set the option *pwfeedback*. Don't use this option if you can squirm out of it; anyone watching the user type will learn the length of their password.

Alternate Passwords

One of sudo's features is that it demands the user's password to perform privileged actions, rather than the root password. In environments with certain regulatory compliance requirements, users might need to enter the target user's password rather than their own. (Regulatory compliance drives sysadmins to unimaginable feats of daftness.) Sudo includes options to permit requiring a different account's password.

---

[28] Fortunately, the boss usually gets tired and decides to take a nap before he can log in and do any real damage.

To require the root password rather than the user's, use the *rootpw* option. Consider this sudoers fragment. Users in wheel can run any command they want. If they want to run a command in the SHELL alias, they must enter the root password.

```
Cmnd_Alias SHELL=/bin/sh, /bin/bash, /usr/bin/su
Defaults!SHELL rootpw
%wheel ALL=ALL
```

To demand the target user's password when running `sudo -u`, use the *targetpw* option. SUSE Linux uses this by default.

Finally, the *runaspw* option tells sudo to demand the password of the default RunAs user. You might want users who run any programs as the **mysql** user to use the **mysql** account's password rather than their own.

```
Defaults>mysql runaspw
```

These options all work, but increase the chances of user confusion and thus the number of helpdesk tickets you'll get. Reduce your workload by offering users a little guidance about what password they must use, as discussed in "Customizing the Password Prompt" in a page or two.

Failure Responses

Sudo traditionally insults users when they failed to type their password correctly. While insulting users has long been considered a sysadmin prerogative, many companies consider it unprofessional to do so to the user's face. Even organizations that allow such insults usually prefer that the sysadmin perform said insults in person, rather than automating the job with sudo's *insults* option. Sudo therefore offers workplace-friendly messages for mistyped passwords.

Each time the user fails to type their password, sudo replies with "Sorry, try again." Change this message with *badpass_message*.

If the user fails all of their permitted authentication attempts, sudo says "sudo: 3 incorrect password attempts." Change this with the *authfail_message* option. The escape character %d gives the number of failed password attempts.

Consider this snippet of senior sysadmin Thea's sudoers policy.

```
Defaults !insults
Defaults:%wheel insults
Defaults:mike badpass_message=\
   "Nervous? Good! I'm watching you!"
Defaults:mike authfail_message=\
   "You failed to even type your password correctly %d
   times, and think you should have root?"
```

Regular users do not get insulted. Members of **wheel** (sysadmins) are accustomed to being abused by their machines and a lack of insults would only confuse them, so sudo obliges. The senior sysadmin has selected one user for special messages every time he mistypes his password, and a final message when he completely fails to authenticate. It's as if Thea doesn't like me or something.

Customizing the Password Prompt

Sudo's password prompt is exactly what you'd expect from a Unix system. It's effective, simple, and boring. Customize the password prompt at the policy level, or at the user level.

Custom Prompts via Policy

Use the *passprompt* option to set a custom password prompt.

```
Defaults passprompt=\
   "Enter your feeble password, if you dare:"
```

This is, at best, mildly amusing. Once.

Using escape characters in the password prompt makes the custom prompt useful. Escape characters let you grab information from the local host and your sudoers command and add them to the password prompt. For example, insert the server's short hostname with *%h* and the fully qualified hostname with *%H*.

```
Defaults passprompt="Enter your password for %h: "
```

To name the user whose password sudo expects, use *%p*. This tells users what password to enter when you're using options like *rootpw*, *runaspw*, and *targetpw*.

```
Defaults passprompt="Enter %p's password on %h: "
```

To name the user the command will run as, use *%U*. If your users frequently run commands as users other than root, this can help them keep things straight. To name the user running sudo, use %u. In an environment with a complicated policy, these hints help everyone.

```
Defaults passprompt=\
    "%u: Enter %p's password to run commands as %U: "
```

If you need a percent sign in your prompt, use two consecutive percent signs *(%%)*.

The *passprompt* option expects that the system's authentication system uses a password prompt of `Password:` or `username's Password:`. Some challenge-response authentication systems and PAM modules use different prompts. A user can also customize their sudo password prompt at the command line. Set the option *passprompt_override* to override these settings and force sudo to always use your prompt.

User Prompt Customization

Users can customize their sudo command prompt at the sudo command line or in their environment.

Use sudo's -p flag to customize the password prompt on a single sudo run. This accepts all the escape characters supported by the sudoers policy password prompt.

```
$ sudo -p "%u: enter %p's password:" -l
```

For a longer-term solution, the environment variable SUDO_PROMPT also lets users set a custom command prompt. It supports the same escape characters. Here's a .profile entry for such a prompt.

```
SUDO_PROMPT="password for %p@%H:" ; export SUDO_PROMPT
```

The SUDO_PROMPT environment variable overrides any custom prompt set by the policy, so if you use it you might be concealing important hints offered by your sysadmin. I recommend including *%p* in your prompt, so you'll at least get a hint about what password sudo expects.

Effective and Expiration Dates

Theoretically, when a new sysadmin joins the team they get a user account and you configure sudo access for that account. On occasion, though, a user might temporarily need privileged access to commands. In most organizations, this means changing the policy when the project begins and changing it again once the project ends. If your organization has strict policy controls, however, you might need to hard-code these dates in the policy.

Sudo sets rule activation and expiration with the NOTBEFORE and NOTAFTER tags. A rule becomes valid at the time set in NOTBEFORE. It still works at the exact time given in NOTAFTER, but expires instantly afterwards.

Sudo uses a time format of a four-digit year, followed by two digits each for month, day, hour, minute, second, and a one-digit tenth of a second—or, *YYYYMMDDHHMMSST*. This defaults to the system time zone. To use UTC times on a host set to the local time, add a Z to the end of the time. If you want a time other than the local time zone or UTC, add an offset like -0800 to the end of the time. Minutes, seconds and fractions of seconds are optional; if you don't include them, they're assumed to be zero. For example, eight AM on 23 February 2021 is 2021022308, while eight-thirty that day is 202102230830.

Here, contractor Karl has unrestricted access for the month of July 2021.

```
karl ALL = NOTBEFORE=2019070100 NOTAFTER=201907312359 ALL
```

A rule with a nonexistent date never gets used. If Thea grants me full access to her systems for the whole day of 30 February, it never works.

In an LDAP policy, setting *sudoers_timed* in `ldap.conf` enables the sudoNotBefore and sudoNotAfter attributes. The date format works exactly like NOTBEFORE and NOTAFTER. Be careful, though: sudo interprets these times in the most permissive manner possible, using the earliest matching sudoNotBefore and the latest sudoNotAfter. If you have two similar sudoRoles for a user, but one grants access for the first ten days of September and another for the last ten days of October, that user gets access for the entirety of September and October. Remove obsolete sudoNotBefore and sudoNotAfter sudoRoles from your directory.

Selectively Disabling Authentication

Sometimes you want a user to have the ability to run a command without using a password. If you're always reconfiguring your laptop to connect to different networks, it might make sense to not bother with a password for dhclient(8), ifconfig(8), and related commands. Running select commands without a password makes sense for accounts dedicated to automated tasks.

Broadly disabling sudo authentication is unwise. Yes, it's certainly convenient. Also, any intruder or application that gets a command prompt or access to your account also gains total access to all of your sudo privileges. If you're running a Linux variant that gives the first user full root access via sudo, then the rogue process will completely own your machine. Do you lock your desktop or log out of your SSH sessions when you go out for lunch? If not, anyone who walks up to your computer can inflict any damage they like on your servers. Disabling sudo authentication is equivalent to deliberately implementing the Windows 95 security system.[29] I prefer the pain of managing authentication to the pain of explaining to the CEO why my account destroyed the web server. If you don't want to bother entering a password when you need sudo, look at alternative authentication mechanisms via PAM as discussed later this chapter.

The *authenticate* option enables user authentication. You don't see it often because it's an invisible global default. Negate it to disable authentication on certain commands. Here I disable authentication for networking-related commands.

```
Cmnd_Alias NETWORK = /sbin/ifconfig, /sbin/dhclient
Defaults!NETWORK, !authenticate
```

I can now set up my laptop to work at the coffee shop without worrying about nosy kids peering over my shoulder at my password.

You can also use the tags PASSWD and NOPASSWD in your sudoers policy. While you'll rarely see the PASSWD tag, use NOPASSWD to disable authentication on a rule.

```
pete dbtest1 = (pg) NOPASSWD: /opt/pg/bin/*
```

Pete can use sudo to run any Postgres command as the user **pg** on the host **dbtest1** without entering a password.

---

29 For those readers too young to remember: Windows 95 had no security system.

Authentication Caching and Timeouts

Sudo remembers the date and time of your last successful authentication in each terminal session. When you run sudo a second time in the same terminal, sudo checks the timestamp. If the timestamp is sufficiently recent, it permits you to run sudo without authentication. You can control how sudo treats this cache and how old a timestamp suffices for authentication.

Configuring Timeouts

Run `sudo -V` as **root** and search for the string "timestamp" to get current settings.

```
# sudo -V | grep timestamp
Authentication timestamp timeout: 5.0 minutes
Path to authentication timestamp dir: /var/run/sudo/ts
Type of authentication timestamp record: tty
```

The authentication timestamp is good for five minutes. Once you enter your password in a given terminal, you won't need to enter it again for five minutes. The timestamps are stored in */var/run/sudo/ts*, and are recorded on a per-terminal basis.

Change the life of the authentication timestamp with the *timestamp_timeout* option. Set it to a number of minutes, or 0 to require a password every time people run sudo.

`Defaults timestamp_timeout=0`

Change the location of the timestamp directory with *timestamp_dir*, and the owner of those files with *timestamp_owner*, but they really need to be in a location that gets recreated every time the system boots. A filesystem like */var/run* is perfect for timestamps.

Erasing Timeouts

To totally remove the authentication timestamp from all of your sessions, run `sudo -K`. This either removes your timestamps or, if it can't remove the file, sets them to 31 December 1969. Wipe your timestamps before leaving your desk—remember, knowledgeable folks can overcome most lock screens. You don't want someone like me unlocking your workstation and using your access.

Sometimes you don't want to erase all of your timestamps, but only those in your current session. This is especially useful when testing and debugging sudo policies or authentication configuration. Use `sudo -k` to wipe the timestamp for only the terminal you run it in.

Multi-Session Authentication

Sudo includes the terminal device in the authentication timestamp. This lets sudo determine which terminal window you've authenticated in. Assume I SSH into a server twice, using terminals `/dev/pts/81` and `/dev/pts/82`. I must authenticate in both terminal sessions.

Many people find this strange. It's really hard to isolate two processes owned by the same user from each other. Users have complete control over their own processes, after all.

Some operating systems configure sudo to permit sharing authentication between terminal sessions. If you open two SSH sessions to a server and authenticate to sudo in one session, the other session can use the same authentication timestamp.

This means that if a skilled intruder penetrates a user account while the user is active in another session, the intruder can use tracers and debuggers to run commands via sudo so long as any terminal session has a valid timestamp. Requiring separate authentication for each terminal window increases the skill an attacker needs to further penetrate the system—your average script kiddie won't have the expertise needed to hijack another terminal's sudo session.

Control per-terminal authentication with the *ttytickets* option. Negating this option lets multiple terminals share a single authentication timestamp. Unless you have very strong reasons for disabling per-terminal timestamps, however, I encourage you to leave them in place.

Authentication, Updates, and Queries

Sudo has two user functions that don't run commands. The `-l` flag tells sudo to print out the user's sudo policy, so the user can see what they have access to. The `-v` flag updates the user's authentication timestamp. Users must enter their password to use these functions, but you can configure the policy to only require that password under specific conditions. The *listpw* option controls authentication required to list sudo privileges, while *verifypw* controls the authentication needed to update the timestamp.

Setting these options to *all* tells sudo to demand a password unless none of the user's permitted commands require a password. If Lucy doesn't need to enter a password to run any of the backup jobs she's responsible for, and both options are set to *all*, she can update her timestamp or list her privileges without a password. A user who can use some commands without authentication, but must enter a password for other commands, must enter a password to update their timestamp. The option *verifypw* defaults to *all*.

To disable asking for a password if a user can use even one command without authentication, use *any*. This is the default for *listpw*. The example earlier where you set your laptop to not need authentication to configure the network? In a default configuration, it lets anyone list your sudo privileges.

To always demand a password, regardless of any other policy decisions, set *verifypw* to *always*.

To allow listing privileges or updating the timestamp without a password, set the option to *never*.

This policy requires a password to list permissions for every user except Thea. It also permits users who can run even one command without a password to update their timestamp without a password, but only on host **www**.

```
Defaults listpw=always
Defaults:thea listpw=never
Defaults@www verifypw=any
```

Changing the *listpw* and *verifypw* options for commands or RunAs doesn't make much sense, but you can change them for hosts and users.

Lecturing Users

Chapter 5 uses sudo's famous lecture in several examples, but let's discuss the lecture in more detail. The "lecture" is the message displayed the first time a user authenticates to sudo on a host.

```
We trust you have received the usual lecture from the
local System Administrator. It usually boils down to
these three things:

    #1) Respect the privacy of others.
    #2) Think before you type.
    #3) With great power comes great responsibility.
```

You then get a chance to enter your password. This is a reasonable general warning, but the *lecture* and *lecture_file* options let you more finely target your hectoring of users.

The *lecture* option sets when the user gets lectured. The default, *once*, tells sudo to give each user the lecture once, on first use, and never again. Using *always* tells sudo to lecture the user each and every time, while using *never* or *!lecture* entirely disables the lecture.

If you want to give a personalized lecture for certain hosts, commands, or users, set *lecture_file* to the path to a file containing the lecture.

Here, Thea has set a customized lecture for any host in the PRODUCTION alias. It's given any time anyone runs sudo, and presumably has stern warnings about sysadmin oversight and the change control process. In the second rule, I get my own lecture.

```
Defaults@PRODUCTION lecture=always, \
    lecture_file=/etc/sudo/prod-lecture
Defaults:mike lecture=always, \
    lecture_file=/etc/sudo/jerk
```

My personal lecture file might contain something like this.

```
Everything you do is logged.
And Thea studies the logs.
I'm on to you, mister.
```

I'm wounded—nay, *hurt*—that she doesn't trust me.

PAM and Sudo

Passwords are cruddy authentication tokens. Most users create terrible passwords, and a sufficiently dedicated intruder can guess them. Most everyone knows that they should have unique passwords for every service, but very few people manage it. Adding another layer of authentication to your privileged processes, or eliminating passwords in favor of another system, can improve your security.

Most Unixes manage authentication through Pluggable Authentication Modules, or PAM. PAM is notoriously complicated, and multiple competing PAM implementations make it outright treacherous. Just as this is not a book on LDAP, this is not a book on PAM. This section probably contains enough clues so that you can get my example working on your system (perhaps with some additional research), but it won't make you into a PAM wizard. If you're not familiar with PAM, I suggest you read my book *PAM Mastery* (Tilted Windmill Press, 2016) before wrecking your PAM configuration. If you want to change how sudo authenticates, however, PAM is how you do it.

Each authentication method comes as a *PAM module*, containing the code to connect that authentication method to the operating system. In addition to the usual password, Unix, Kerberos, and LDAP modules found on most Unix-like systems, you can find PAM modules to implement Google Authenticator, RSA tokens, Windows SMB authentication, and many more. Here, I'm hooking SSH agent authentication into PAM.

An SSH agent runs on the user's desktop computer. It holds a user's decrypted SSH authentication keys in RAM, flagged so they can never be written to swap space on the disk. If the SSH client or session must validate possession of those keys, it asks the desktop agent to perform the validation. This is stronger than password authentication, as the user must have both the key and the passphrase for that key. It is not true two-factor authentication, but is less bad than passwords.

The PAM module pam_ssh_agent_auth (http://pamsshagentauth.sourceforge.net/) permits PAM authentication against your SSH agent. I'll use this module as an example of changing sudo's authentication method.

Prerequisites

Before configuring sudo to use SSH agent authentication, verify that your system is suitable for it.

Your SSH client must forward your desktop SSH agent to the server, and the server must accept the agent forwarding. Many organizations disallow this. Check your environment for the variable SSH_AUTH_SOCK. If it doesn't exist, or is set to anything except a file path, agent forwarding is not working.

Now install pam_ssh_agent_auth. Unlike much modern software, it has no compile-time options. If your operating system has a packaged version, use it.

Authenticating to an SSH agent requires passing the $SSH_AUTH_SOCK environment variable through sudo. You'll probably need other SSH environment variables as well, so I'd recommend you keep everything beginning with SSH_. Also, once agent authentication works sudo can easily double-check your authentication every time you run it. Sudo won't need to keep timestamps. Disable them.

```
Defaults env_keep += "SSH_*", timestamp_timeout=0
```

Once you have all this, configure the PAM module on a disposable test machine. Be sure you keep a privileged terminal open throughout the testing process, and that you have the actual root password available for recovery.

Configuring PAM

PAM keeps its configuration in system directories like */etc/pam.d* or */usr/local/etc/pam.d*. A PAM-aware program looks for its configuration in these directories, in a file named after the program. Look for a file named *sudo*.

PAM policies include up to four different types of rules: auth, account, session, and password. Each rule calls a PAM module like pam_unix, pam_ldap, pam_mkhomedir, and so on.

The PAM module pam_unix handles traditional password authentication. Find an auth rule in sudo's PAM configuration that calls that module. The specifics vary between Unixes, but it'll have both "auth" and pam_unix" like this example.

```
auth    required    pam_unix.so    no_warn try_first_pass nullok
```

If that rule doesn't exist, look for a PAM auth rule that sucks in the main system authentication.

```
auth            include         system
```

These rules both tell sudo to authenticate with passwords. To use SSH agent authentication rather than passwords, replace this rule.

```
auth sufficient pam_ssh_agent_auth.so file=~/.ssh/authorized_keys
```

This horrible string means that authenticating with the method in the shared library pam_ssh_agent_auth.so is sufficient to log onto the host. You might need to give the full path to the file `pam_ssh_agent_auth.so`, depending on how your operating system installs new PAM libraries and how your PAM implementation finds them. At the end of the rule, the argument *file=* gives the path to the user's `authorized_keys` file. Add any additional arguments to the end of the rule.

Save the changes to sudo's PAM policy. Sudo should now be able to authenticate against your SSH agent. Open a new terminal window that hasn't yet used sudo and try it.

```
$ sudo touch /tmp/test
```

If sudo prompts you for a password and waits for you to enter it, you haven't removed your password policy. If sudo prompts you for a password three times in a row without giving you a chance to enter one, and immediately displays a failure message, sudo is using the PAM module but cannot connect to your SSH agent. Check your agent forwarding. I'll often set an authentication failure message as a reminder. Sudo only needs one attempt to authenticate when using SSH agent authentication, so I reduce the number of password attempts to 1.

```
Defaults passwd_tries=1,authfail_message="SSH Agent?."
```

If you still have trouble, configure auth logging in `sudo.conf` and add the *debug* flag to the pam_ssh_agent_auth PAM rule.

authorized_keys Location

Many enterprises do not let their users own their own `authorized_keys` file on servers. Rather than letting users update their own key files directly, key file updates go through a central management system like Ansible or Puppet that copies them to all the servers simultaneously. Such key files do not reside in the user's home directory. You need to tell pam_ssh_agent_auth where to find them.

The pam_ssh_agent_auth supports several escape characters for this purpose. The tilde (~) and *%h* characters both represent the user's home directory. *%H* represents the short hostname, without the domain name, while *%f* means the fully qualified domain name. Finally, *%u* represents the username.

Suppose you stored the keys in `/etc/sshkeys/`, where each user's authorized keys are put in a file named after their user account.

```
auth sufficient pam_ssh_agent_auth.so file=/etc/sshkeys/%u
```

The pam_ssh_agent_auth module thinks that files outside the user's home directory should be owned by **root**. It's a reasonable assumption—either the key files are owned by the user, or they're owned by the system. If a user can write to key files outside their home directory, set the option *allow_user_owned_authorized_keys_file* in the PAM auth rule to tell the module to accept such permissions on the files.

This isn't the only possible PAM configuration for sudo. By tweaking PAM rules you could require both a password and an SSH agent. You could add Google Authenticator to the mix, or authenticate via gene testing once you find the module. If a PAM module exists for your operating system, you can plug it into sudo.

And given this, you can now make sudo do anything it's capable of.

There is NOOO… Chapter Six!

Afterword

You now know more about sudo than the vast majority of people who didn't write it. Congratulations! But there's always more to learn. If you have a weird problem, check the sudo web site at https://sudo.ws, the sudo man pages, and the archives of the sudo-users mailing list. Sudo has been successfully deployed on millions of very different systems, and it can work for you too.

Probably.

Sudo might not be the solution for your specific problem. Some applications expect to own the server, and trying to restrict them is futile at best. If you manage your organization by running shell scripts as root, running those same shell scripts with sudo will leave unauthorized users lots of ways to escalate their privileges. Some problems are too large for sudo to fix.

And the next time someone tells you that "Sudo is how you get root," treat them to a short sharp visit from the Slap Fairy.

Sponsors

I offer people the opportunity (for very exploitative values of "opportunity") to sponsor my books. They send me money before the book is finished, and I put their name in the book. Sponsors provide me financial stability as I'm writing, and have more than once bailed me out of a tight spot. If you're interested in suffering this sort of exploitation, see https://mwl.io to sign up for my sponsor mailing list.

The following fine folks made writing this book a whole bunch easier.

Print Sponsors

Bob Eager
tanamar corporation
Rogier Krieger
Todd Miller
Philip Vuchetich
Chris Dunbar
Stefan Johnson
Trix Farrar
Niall Navin
Trond Endrestøl
Russell Folk
Roman Zolotarev
Phi Network Systems
Andreas Eberli
Lucas Raab
Cal Ledsham
Ross Williams

Patronizers

If you think sponsorships are a ripoff, wait until you get a load of my Patreon. For an ongoing monthly payment, you can get copies of everything I write or your name in books. It's a terrible deal. Despite this, Patronizers Kate Ebneter, Jeff Marraccini, Stefan Johnson, and Phillip Vuchetich bribe me to get their name in the print version of every book.

Comparing the list of Patronizers to the list of sponsors, I see that the overlap is non-zero. Apparently I'm not screaming "this is a ripoff" loudly enough.

In all sincerity, I thank every one of you. For letting me rip you off.

Never miss a new Lucas release!

Sign up for Michael W Lucas' mailing lists.
https://mwl.io

.	 126
-	 126
=	3,82,102,153
/	 104
\	 41
!	 41,71-73,76,78-81,84,89,105-106,
	 111,112,116,118,130-132,134,137,
	141-144,153-154,158-159,177,
	187-188,192,196
[(1)	 126
+	61,63-64,157
+=	82,102-106,113,141,155,199
-=	 82,102-104,
:	 65-66,79
::1	63,138
@	62,79,118,141,144,154,196-197
>	81,179
<	 179
/ (directory divider)	 56
%	 41,51,59-60,63-66,68,71,81,84-86,
	...105,123,129-130,138,141,143-145,154,
	 157,171,177,187
%d	41,188
%f	 201
%h	51,189,201
%H	41,189,201
%p	 189-190
%u	 189-190,201
%U	 189
%#	 60
%:	 61
%:#	 61
"" (wildcard)	 57
%d	 41
%h	 51
%H	 41
?	 54-55,57
*	55-57
#	 41,60-61
#include	 41,50-52
	protecting 50
#includedir	 41,51-52
	protecting 52
.login	 109
.profile	109,190
10baseT	 90
127.0.0.1	63,138

access control list	.................................see ACL
accountability	 23
ACL	19-20,22,163,175
Active Directory	 53,60,149,151
AIX	 148
aliases	57-59
	expanding 144-145
ALL	40-42,44-46,50-51,54-58,60-73,81-87,
	89-90,105,107,111,117,123,129-130,
	 134-136,138,141,143-144,152,154,
	 156,158-159,171,187,191
ALLCOMMANDS	 70-72,138
always_set_home (option)	 112
Ansible	36,48-49,139,201
askpass	 115-116
asterisk	.... see *
authenticate (option)	 192
authentication	20-22,26,32,34-35,77,78,
	 80,94,100,105,149,161,164,168,
	 173-174,185-201
	caching 193
	disabling 191-192
	LDAP 149,161,164
	multisession 194-195
	timeout 193-194
authfail_message (option)	188,200
authority	 26
authorized_keys	 200-201
automation	 50
awk(1)	 169
backup_alias.pl	 131-132
BADCOMMANDS	70-71
badpass_message (option)	78,187-188
bash	36,71-73,100,130,134,141,143-145,
	153,183,187
	functions 103
BECOME_ROOT	71-73
bg(1)	 117
bickering	 23
blood sacrifices	 161
bridge	 63
BSD	24,45
cd	 101
CentOS	 24-25,30,45,125,149
cheat	 128
checksum	....see "Digest"
CIFS	 53

Cmnd_Alias ... 57-59,67,70-72,80,86,118,124,
............127-131,141,143-144,177,187,192
CNAME 137
COLORS 102-104
COLORTERM 103
command.. 38
    Defaults 80-81
command alias 57,59,67-71,86,90,111,
.... 124-131,134,145,152,171
    ALL is dangerous 68-69,90,134
command list..66-67
    negation...71-73
command_timeout (option) 117-119,
.... 141-144,153-155,159,163
comments 41
compactness 40
compress_io.. 180
console 63
core dumps 95-96,98
createall.pl...69-70
cryptographic digest......................see "Digest"
CTRL-Z... 117
cvtsudoers................... 15,33,140,142-146,153,
....155,160,164
cvtsudoers.conf....................... 145-146,153
CWD 177-178

dd(1)... 121
Debian............ 24-25,30,34,45,49,124-125,149
Debug... 95,173-174
debugging 32,172-174
Defaults (sudoers) 46,75,78-82
    conflicting..81-82
    per-command....................................80-81
    per-host...79-80
    per-RunAs.. 81
    per-user...78-79
dhclient(8) 191-192
digest 121-132,134,158,
    automating................................... 124-132
    computing................................... 122-123
    in sudoers................................... 123-124
DISPLAY... 102
Distinguished Name................... 151,157
DNS 63
    in sudoers................................... 136-138
doas(1) 22
DOOM 112
Domain Admins 53

Domain Name Service.......................see DNS
DTrace.. 174

ed(1) 45,75
editing privileged files.............................87-88
editor (option)...................................... 46,75
EDITOR (environment variable) 46,88,100
EDOOFUS... 99
elegance, lacking 164
emacs.. 45,75
email 170-172
env(1) 99,113
environment
    customizing 110
    dangerous.. 100-101
    execution... 101
    filtering................................... 103-106
    per-rule 105
    sanitizing................................... 103-104
    standard sudo 104-105
    variables 99-119
env_check (option)................103-104,106,110
env_delete (option) 106,113
env_editor (option) 46
env_file (option) 109-110,113
env_keep (option) 46,82,102-106,110,
.... 141-145,155,163,199
env_reset.. 106,112
EVERYTHING 128-130
EXEC (tag) 67,85-86,131,141,143-145,154
exploitation..205,207

facility (syslog) 35,168
federal regulations 97
fnmatch(3) 53
FOLLOW (tag) 88-89
fqdn (option).. 63,137
FreeBSD 24-25,34-35,86,96,124,
....128-129,131,149
fs.suid_dumpable... 96
FTP_PROXY 82,110
fully qualified domain names 136-137,189

gentleman's agreements ....see "Debacle"
GID 41,61
github.. 97,125
glob(3) 53
Google Authenticator 198
group ID .... see GID

groups 28-29,65-66
    large numbers of 95
    non-Unix 62
    operating system 60
    and LDAP 152
group_source (option) 60
G_BROKEN_FILENAMES 99

hamster 75
happy 49
hardware token 185
hash mark 41
hash, cryptographic .... see "Digest"
HOME 82,100-101,104,110,112
homogenous network 49
host 38
host aliases 64-65
Host_Alias 59,64-65,138-139,141,143
host lists 63-65
host.conf 137
hostname(1) 39,63
HOSTNAME 104
hostnames 136-138
HTTP_PROXY 82,100,110

id(1) 29,60
ifconfig(8) 26,83,191-192
IFS 100
ignore_dot (option) 111
ignore_iolog_errors 176
ignore_unknown_defaults (option) ....
.... 139-140
include .... see #include
includedir .... see #includedir
insults (option) 76-78,81,140,187-188
intrusion detection 31
iolog_dir (option) 176
iolog_flush (option) 180
IP addresses 63-64
I/O logging 174-184
    log rotation 183-184
    searching 180-183

Java Server Pages 36
JSON 140,142

KDE 179
Kerberos 102
kern.nosuidcoredump 96

kern.sugid_coredump 96
konsole(1) 179
KRB5CCNAME 102

LANG 102-103
LANGUAGE 102-103
last match ....
.... 43,45,50,64,82,138-139,152,156,159
LC_* 102-103
LDAP 22,25,31,37,59,63,66,68,118,
....137,140,146-165,173-174,191,197,198
    administrator .. 148,150-151,153,162,164
    policy container 151
    schema 150-151
ldapadd(1) 150
ldap.conf 161,191
ldap.secret 161
ldap_conf 161
ldap_secret 161
LDIF 140,142,148-149,151,153,155-156,
.... 158,160,164
ldifde 151
LD_ 100
LD_LIBRARY_PATH 106,108,110
LD_LIBRARY_PRELOAD 85,100
LD_PRELOAD 85,
lecture (option) 79-81,196-197
lecture_file (option) 80,196-197
less(1) 83-85,87,112-113,134
LESSSECURE 113
lexical order 52
license, sudo 23-24
Lightweight Directory Access Protocol ....
.... see "LDAP"
line printers 99
LINGUAS 102-103
Linux 18,20,24,96-97,99,109,122,125,
.... 127-128,187,192
listpw (option) 195-196
localhost 63,137-138
logging 32
LOGNAME 101,104
log_output (option) 176-177
LOG_OUTPUT (tag) 177
LS_COLORS 102
ls(1) 83

macOS 22,24,30
MAIL (environment variable) 101,104

Entry	Page(s)
MAIL (tag)	171
mail	32
mailfrom (option)	170-171
mailsub (option)	170-171
mailto (option)	170-171
mail_all_cmnds (option)	171
mail_always (option)	171
mail_badpass (option)	171
mail_no_host (option)	171
mail_no_perms (option)	171
mail_no_user (option)	171
malfeasance	72,169
MANPAGER	113
match	145
max_groups (option)	60
MAYEXEC	86,141,143-144
Mens, JP	48,139
Microsoft NTFS	20
Miller, Todd	15,
Minix	24
mksnap_ffs(8)	66
Monty Python	15,
more(1)	83
mount(8)	26
mv(1)	121
MySQL	68
Nagios	84
negation	41,71-73,152,158
negotiating	26
netgroup	61,64
netgroup_tuple (option)	61
newaliases(8)	86,124,131,141,143,145
newfs(8)	26
NFS	175-176
NFSv4	20,175
NIS	61,64,66
NOEXEC (tag)	67,69,81,85,87,118, 129-130,134
and static binaries	86-87
NOEXEC (option)	85-86,134,141,143-145, 154-155,159,163
NOFOLLOW (tag)	89
nohup(1)	117
nolog_output (option)	177
NOLOG_OUTPUT (tag)	177
NOMAIL (tag)	171
NOPASSWD (tag)	67,192
NOTAFTER (tag)	190-191
NOTBEFORE (tag)	190-191
nsswitch.conf	137,148-149,162,165
obsessed toddlers	72
One Identity	97
OpenBSD	22,49
OpenLDAP	149-151,161
OpenSolaris	21,24
OpenSSH	115-116
openssh-askpass(1)	115
openssl	123
options	76-78
output_format	145
PAGER	113
pagers	112-113
PAM	34-35,94,109,185,189,192,197-201
pam_env	109
pam_ldap	199
pam_mkhomedir	199
pam_ssh_agent_auth	198-201
pam_unix	199
passprompt (option)	188-189
passprompt_override (option)	189
passwd (1)	19,67,111,116,121,122-123, 158,167-168,178-179,183
passwd_timeout (option)	186
passwd_tries (option)	77,185-186
PASSWD (tag)	192
password	185-187
alternate	186-187
expiration	190-191
number of attempts	185-186
prompt	188-190
timeouts	185-186
PATH	99-104,111,121
Path	95,97,115
Perl	53,69-71,124,126-129,131
PGDATABASE	108
PGHOST	108
PGPASSFILE	108
pitfalls	30
Pluggable Authentication Modules	see PAM
plugins	96-98
Plugin (keyword)	95-98
plugin_dir	95,97
policy	30
policy distribution	31

posixGroup	157
posixUser	157
Postgres	21,68,105,108,192
poudriere	149
priority (syslog)	168
Privilege Manager for Sudo	97
probe_interfaces	95
proxy server	110
psql	36
PS1	102
PS2	102
PS4	106,
Puppet	48,139,201
pwfeedback (option)	186
rdist(1)	133
README.LDAP	148
reboot(8)	39-41,61,176-177
reinstalling	27
requiretty (option)	116
responsibility	26
restricted_env_file (option)	109-110
root, eliminating	29-30
rootpw (option)	187
RSA tokens	198
rsync(1)	133
rsyslog	170
RunAs	65-66
runaspw (option)	187
RunAs_Alias	59,66,141
sandwich	15-16,22
scorpion pit	63
secure_path (option)	111
sed(1)	169
Sendmail	84,123
sendmail(8)	86,124
service(8)	39,50
session logging	174-184
Set	95-96
setenv (option)	107
SETENV (tag)	107-108
setgid	19-20,28
setuid	19-20
sewage	20
SHA digests	122-123
sha512 (digest)	123-124,128,158
sha512(1)	122
sha512sum(1)	123

SHELL (environment)	99,101,104
shell escape	83-85,87,90
shell scripts	134
shells, running with sudo	113-115
shell_noargs	114
shenanigans	143
shutdown	176-177
silly	147
slapd(8)	150
slapd.conf	150
Solaris	109
SHLVL	99
Slap Fairy	203
SLIP	99
SSH	62,83-84,102-103,105,141-145,155,
	163,185,192,194,198-201
SSH agent	185,198-201
SSH_AUTH_SOCK	102,198-199
SSH_CLIENT	102
SSH_CONNECTION	102
SSH_TTY	102
sssd(8)	162,165,173
su(1)	19,22,29-30,60,71-73,81-82,111,
	113-114,118,130,141,143-145,
	153,183,187
subpoenaed	184
sudo(8)	
-b	117
-g	36,181
-h	47-48
-i	109,111
-k	194
-l	37,42-43,47-48,73,76,84,98,123,
	170,174,190,195
-n	116
-s	114-115
-u	36-37,107,112,187
-A	116
-E	107-108
-H	112
-K	194
-P	37
-T	119
-U	47-48
-V	24,34-35,46,49,93-94,98,102,
	,106,161,170,193
--preserve-env	108
avoiding	28
learning	27

su 113-115
    support 23-24
    what's wrong with 21-23
sudodigest.pl 125,128-129,131-132
sudoedit 71,87-89,94,158,172-174
sudoedit_checkdir (option) 89
sudoedit_follow (option) 88-89
sudoers 33,35,37-90,93-96,98,102,107,
    113,116,122-125,127-128,133,
   135-140,142-145,147-149,151-164,
   168-169,171-174,187-189,192
    changing location of 98
    final rule 45
    grammar version..................................... 49
    LDAP, compared to 151-152
    options ....see "options"
    valid 45
    validate 48-49
    invalid 49
sudoers_base 153,161-162
sudoers_debug 162
sudoers_file 98
sudoers_gid 98
sudoers_mode 98
sudoers_search_filter 161-162
sudoers_timed 161,191
sudoers_uid 98
sudoers.ldap(5) 148
sudoreplay(8) 33,89,175-183
    -l 181-183
    -m 179
    -s 179-182
sudoCommand 156,158-159
sudoHost 156-158
sudoOption 155,158-159,163
sudoOrder 152-153,156,158-160
sudoRole 155-160,163-164,191
sudoRunAsGroup............................... 158-159
sudoRunAsUser 158-159
sudoUser 150,156-157
sudo.conf ...60,93-95,98,115,161,172-174,200
SUDO_COMMAND 99
SUDO_EDITOR (environment variable) ......
   46,88
SUDO_GID.. 99-100
SUDO_UID... 99-100
SUDO_USER 99-100
sudo_pair 97-98
sudo.schema 150

SUSE 20,187
static binary 86,134
sysadmin sausage... 105
syslog 35,167-170,172,174-175,179
syslog (option) 168
syslogng 170
syslog_badpri (option)................................ 168
syslog_goodpri (option) 168
syslog_maxlen (option) 169
system security services daemon ....see "sssd"

tail(1) 117-118
targetpw (option)... 187
tcsh 36
TERM 101,103-104
terminals.. 115-116
TIMEOUT... 117,154
timeouts
    command 117-118
    erasing 194
    user 119
timestamp_dir (option) 193
timestamp_owner (option) 193
timestamp_timeout (option) ....
   77-78,80,193,199
torment 48
truss 174
TZ 103,110
ttytickets (option)... 195

Ubuntu..22,30,44
UID 41,61,100,157
USER 101,104,178
user aliases..58-59,62-63
user ID .... see UID
user lists 59-63
User_Alias 58-59,63,71,141,143-144
user_command_timeout (option)............. 119
username 36,38
users
    running commands as 40

Vallat, Miod... 15
verifypw (option)................................ 195-196
vi(1) 45,-46,75,83,87
vigr(8) 28,43
violence 53
vipw(8) 43
vindictive pleasure.. 26

virtual interfaces 63
   large numbers of 95
VISUAL (environment variable) 46,88,100
visudo(8) 33,43-46,48-52,55,84-86,118,
   131,139-141,143-145,153-154,
   159,173-174
   e 44
   x 44
   Q 45
   ? 45
   -c 48-49,52
   -f 48,51-52
   -q 48-49
   -s 48-49,52
VLAN 63

whitespace 41
wildcards 53-57
   risks 56-57
Windows 101,192,198

X 102
XAUTHORITY 102
XAUTHORIZATION 102
XKCD 22

YP 64,137

Lightning Source UK Ltd.
Milton Keynes UK
UKHW050413270821
389480UK00008BA/550/J